EXPERT
MOTORCYCLING

WILLIAM HAMPTON

Contemporary Books, Inc.
Chicago

Library of Congress Cataloging in Publication Data

Hampton, William.
  Expert motorcycling.

  Includes index.
  1.   Motorcycling.   I.   Title.
GV1059.5.H36   796.7'5   79-50978
ISBN 0-8092-7195-8
ISBN 0-8092-7193-1 pbk.

Published by Contemporary Books, Inc.
180 North Michigan Avenue, Chicago, Illinois 60601
Manufactured in the United States of America
Library of Congress Catalog Card Number: 79-50978
International Standard Book Number: 0-8092-7195-8 (cloth)
                                    0-8092-7193-1 (paper)

Published simultaneously in Canada by
Beaverbooks
953 Dillingham Road
Pickering, Ontario L1W 1Z7
Canada

To Bill Hartford of *Popular Mechanics*

Contents

Introduction

Welcome to *Expert Motorcycling*.

You may be wondering if this book has anything of value for you. Can it *help* you really become an expert motorcyclist? You won't know the answer to that question until you've gone through this book, will you?

Now this book is quite different from most other books that deal with motorcycling in that it delves into certain concepts and riding techniques that at first may seem strange. But, given a fair trial, you'll find that they can *help* you develop your motorcycling skills.

Besides, does it really matter how odd something may appear, if it produces results?

The chapters in this book have been so designed as to provide a series of stepping stones to give you a basic understanding about the various but nonetheless interrelated aspects of motorcycling.

For instance, at the outset, you'll see why the motorcycle

can be the safest vehicle on the road. You're shown how to condition yourself mentally and physically for the rigors of road and off-roading riding.

Additional chapters discuss how to choose the proper protective riding gear, how the motorcycle steers or handles, how to set up your bike so it seems a part of you, and how to keep it safe to ride. Chapters 7 and 8 reveal specific techniques of operating the motorcycle, along with special riding exercises. Two topics that receive detailed treatment are braking and cornering.

In Chapter 9, you're taken out "on the road" where you learn how to "read" surface conditions, deal with bad weather conditions, select tires, master speed wobbles, ride in groups, and cope with other problems.

Then in Chapter 10, you read about techniques for dealing with other drivers and pedestrians. You see how to avoid drivers who have trouble sharing the road with motorcycles. For night riding, Chapter 11 tells you how to see in the dark and how to be seen. Special methods are detailed for increasing safety at night.

Although much of this book is geared to the road rider, Chapter 12 is an exclusive treatment for the off-road rider. Everything from prepping your bike and utilizing special control exercises to riding on different forms of terrain come under scrutiny here. Even if you're a road rider, you'll find that dirt-riding techniques can help improve your road skills.

Aside from the physical stimuli that motorcycling offers, it yields even more of a spiritual satisfaction, or reawakening of the free spirit within you.

That is one of the primary reasons why this book stresses the mental concepts of motorcycling, for they're the key to your success as a motorcyclist. So, keep an open mind. Learn to make use of any concept or technique that can *help* guide you along the road to *Expert Motorcycling*.

—William Hampton

1

Expert Motorcycling: What's It All About?

If you're a serious motorcyclist, you take pride in your ability to operate a motorcycle skillfully. And whether or not you'll admit it, you think that you're a good rider, one who can make his bike respond to the master's touch. In other words, you want to be an expert.

And you should feel this way. For only by taking pride in your skills and by developing them to the ultimate will you ever achieve that unique and satisfying feeling of "master of the motorcycle."

Even if you've yet to straddle a motorcycle and feel that current throbbing through your body, you want to feel that you'll be able to make that mechanical animal respond to your will.

If you're to become an expert rider, you must learn how to master your motorcycle. *If you don't, it will master you.* That's when you get into trouble. A dangerous situation will arise, and if you're not prepared, you won't have total control of your bike.

So right at the outset of your motorcycling career, decide that you're going to be master of your bike. Moreover, if you've been riding for some time but have never learned how to make your bike do your bidding, resolve right now that you're going to be in command.

Master your motorcycle, but do so *respectfully*.

Note that *respectfully*. It's one of the keys to your success as a motorcyclist.

You see, there are two ways to master your bike. The right way is to approach the matter with a mature, common-sense attitude. With this method, you'll respect the motorcycle for the potentially dangerous vehicle it is. And you'll undertake any means possible that'll help you become an expert, without exposing yourself to needless danger.

Now if you're a reckless individual, you can still become an expert rider. But would you care to make a guess how long you'll go before your luck runs out? If fate is kind, you'll be lucky and come away from a close call with nothing more than a realization that you'd better change your reckless ways. Then, too, you may end up as an accident report in the newspaper. The choice is yours.

If you've just started learning to ride, you face some situations that the more-experienced riders have already met. Perhaps these next few sentences will strike home, if you're experiencing some of the problems that each of us goes through in the early stages.

When you're first learning to ride, the two-wheeler seems like a complex, unstable—and to some, frightening—vehicle. Your lack of familiarity with the steel steed keeps you in check. You're afraid to extend yourself, so you're cautious. But then as you gain skill, your confidence increases, too. You find the responsiveness of your motorcycle gives you the false impression that you're more skilled than you really are. What's more, if you don't come to recognize overconfidence, you expose yourself to danger simply by overextending yourself. You think you're a better rider than you really are.

Take a few moments and think about your own attitude. Are you overconfident? Do you take unnecessary chances? Be honest with your self-appraisal, because it's your life on the line.

To become even more aware of what you're up against as a novice, consider this fact: *nearly seventy percent of all motorcycle accidents occur to those individuals who have been riding less than six months.* Read that again. It might seem frightening, but it's not meant to be. It just means that a lot of riders get careless. Even an experienced rider can get hurt, if he gets careless.

Now a motorcycle is no different from any other vehicle in that it depends on the guidance it receives from its operator. Unlike most other vehicles, however, the motorcycle has a lot going for itself. In other words, it's potentially the safest vehicle on the road—*if it's handled properly.* Some may find that hard to believe. But if you're already an expert rider, you're probably nodding your head in agreement.

But if you're not that familiar with bikes, you may be wondering what advantages a motorcycle could have over the enclosed protectiveness of a four-wheeled vehicle.

Well, read on, fellow enthusiast. I'll show you.

First, the motorcycle is inherently stable. At speeds faster than a walking pace, its spinning wheels function like gyroscopes and provide it with an amazing degree of stability. In fact, at high speeds, a motorcycle can steer itself on a straight course. Even if its forward speed diminishes, it will weave from side to side in an effort to stay on two wheels.

When you add this self-stabilization quality to high-traction tires and efficient braking and suspension systems, you can readily see why a properly ridden bike can travel on almost any surface safely.

Further making the motorcycle safe and efficient is the placement of the vital controls. The rear-brake pedal, front-brake lever, clutch lever, and throttle control are so placed that the rider's hands and feet are on—or near—them at all times.

Where to now? With a motorcycle, you have a mechanical magic carpet that can whisk you off to anywhere your heart desires. It's an economical, efficient, and safe way to see different places. *(Courtesy Kawasaki Motor Corp.)*

By having these controls ideally located, you can react to dangerous situations more quickly than the motorist who must lift his foot onto the brake pedal. You can operate both brakes and still have your hand on the throttle, should you need to accelerate quickly.

What's more, with its independent braking systems, the motorcycle has a higher degree of *controlled* stopping power.

When you learn how to operate both brakes together, or independently, you have amazing stopping power.

Another factor making your bike safe and highly maneuverable is due to its single-track nature and small size. You have only to lean your body slightly to change direction. Compare that with the motorist who must turn a slower-reacting steering wheel to turn a larger, less-maneuverable, dual-track vehicle.

Even a car's power steering is no match for a two-wheeler's quick reaction to its operator's sudden shift in body weight.

With your compact, short-wheelbase machine, you can almost turn on a dime to avoid hitting someone's fender. To complement your bike's unequaled agility, you have 360 degree visibility and can see danger approaching from any side. Your field of view isn't hampered by a dirty windshield, doorposts, roof, etc. And when you can spot danger faster than the other guy, you can react more quickly.

Moreover, you're going to stay more mentally refreshed than he is, too, because you'll have a steady flow of fresh air.

When he has his windows rolled up, the car motorist is breathing stale air (okay, maybe he's got air conditioning), listening to the ball game, his wife, six kids, and mother-in-law all at the same time. So, do you think he's as mentally alert as you?

Motorcycle riding is also excellent for sharpening your reflexes, coordination, and timing. When you develop these faculties, they help give you a feeling of oneness with your bike. Your steed becomes an extension of you.

When you get behind the wheel of a car, these faculties that you've honed by cycling help make you a better driver, too.

There's another vital benefit that you acquire as a bike rider: the ability to judge various surface conditions and to ride accordingly. Once you develop this aspect of expert motorcycling, you'll be able to ride on many kinds of surfaces safely. Here again, you'll have something to help you when you drive a car, because you'll have a better feel of the road.

Regardless of the advantages a motorcycle can provide, you must still learn how to use them. That's why this book was written: to help you become an expert rider. Now, no one ever learned how to ride a bike solely from the written word. But it can serve as a useful guide, because you can profit from others' hard-won experience. Many of the techniques in this book have been performed by countless motorcyclists over the years.

If motorcycling really gets into your blood, you'll leave no stone unturned in your quest to become an expert rider. Whether it's getting advice from veteran riders or reading about the latest road tests and technical articles in magazines, you'll seek to add to your storehouse of two-wheeled knowledge and experience.

Motorcycling will open new worlds to you. You'll meet new

people and different situations as you see what life is like from behind handlebars. Life will take on new dimensions.

Ride at your own pace, and don't worry about keeping up with anyone else (unless you get into racing).

Although motorcycling is an individual experience, it can be shared.

There will be many situations in street riding that will place demands on your skill and judgment. Your survival on today's traffic-infested roads means that you'll have to adopt a defensive attitude. There is no other way, believe me. If you are—or become—strictly a dirt rider, you'll encounter challenges different from the street rider that will add to your development as an expert rider.

Regardless where you ride, road or dirt, hopefully this book will help guide you.

2
Are You "Fit" to Ride?

Operating a motorcycle is both a mental and a physical process. In other words, the manner in which your machine performs depends on how well you coordinate your mental and physical faculties.

Your mind has a greater influence on your ability to ride than you may have imagined. Aside from thinking how you're going to operate that piece of machinery, you probably view the maneuvering of it as mostly physical.

But did you know that your subconscious has a tremendous effect on your riding ability?

Before you get bored and skip this chapter, read the next few pages with an open mind.

After all, you want to know all the ins and outs of becoming an expert motorcyclist, don't you? And what if some genie were to suddenly appear to show you how to become that expert on two wheels? Wouldn't it be worth a few minutes of open-minded thinking on your part? Fellow biker,

The racing motorcyclist must have superb riding skills, along with exceptional mental and physical conditioning. *(Courtesy Yamaha International Corp.)*

that genie does exist—in your very own mind. And "it" is just waiting for the chance to spring into action.

Mental Motorcycling

How good a rider you are—or become—depends mostly on your mental attitude.

If you earnestly want to become a better rider, you must believe accordingly. You can call it positive thinking, if you wish.

Now, maybe it's hard for you to accept the fact that thinking about and believing in becoming an expert cyclist can actually help turn you into one. It's true, though. You can prove it to yourself, providing you're willing to give it a fair try.

Of course, it's easy to tell someone to form the right attitude about something. Carrying it out is something else. But if you're to become adept at motorcycling, you must first adopt the proper frame of mind.

Should you have the attitude that a motorcycle is for showing off and operating recklessly, naturally you'll operate it that way. And unless you alter your negative attitude, you'll eventually end up a statistic.

Conversely, if you think of yourself as a good rider who wants to improve even more, you'll find that you'll operate your mount with more skill and safety.

You see, you usually perform something physically according to the deep-seated beliefs you maintain about it. In other words, if you really desire to improve your riding skills, you'll do things that will really improve those skills.

This mode of thinking isn't hard to understand once you accept that your mind possesses a magnetic quality. If it desires something and believes that it's attainable, it'll find ways to bring it about.

Sustaining the right attitude is only part of the means you can use to improve your riding. You can make faster progress by using techniques of visualizing or picturing your thoughts. That is, you must *see* yourself mastering your bike.

You must see yourself in command, as you put it through its paces, smoothly, safely—expertly. If it's a particular maneuver or technique you're trying to master, first find out the right way to go about it. Then perform it in your mind— *successfully*. It's important that you visualize yourself performing properly.

Obviously, you must complement your mental approach with proper physical practice. You still have to operate that bike with your body.

Even without the visualization technique, you can attain skill by practicing with your motorcycle. But by combining the right mental approach with lots of physical practice, your riding skills will improve far more than you ever thought.

Make sure that you only concentrate on what you want to happen. For if you persistently picture the wrong way to do something, your subconscious has no choice but to bring it about. Your subconscious is the creative part of your mind and can't distinguish between what's good or bad for you. Its purpose is to bring to fruition whatever the self-directing part of your mind desires.

When you find yourself operating a motorcycle recklessly, take stock of your attitude. Analyze your outlook toward motorcycling.

To keep yourself from getting too bold, think what can happen when you goof off. Don't dwell on disaster; just think of it occasionally so you realize what harm can befall you when you get out of line.

Another one of the mind's mysterious qualities is its ability to warn of impending disaster. Have you ever had a funny feeling that something was about to happen to you? Well, believe it or not, you can acquire this peculiarity of the mind to sense danger by cultivating an "alert consciousness."

Your desire alone to be an expert rider will help you to recognize and develop abilities that will enhance your alertness. By realizing you're vulnerable to danger, you tend to increase your powers of observation and alertness. You pay more attention to the little things that can warn you of danger: a seemingly harmless wet spot on the road, a car creeping forward at a side-road stop sign as you approach.

In essence, by *willing* yourself to be more alert, your mind develops a sensitivity that can warn you of danger. Your attention will be drawn to that wet spot in the road or to that car about to pull out in front of you. You become more defensive and thereby gear yourself for some kind of accident-preventive action.

Anticipation is another quality that forms an important part of your mental-motorcycling techniques. When you recognize a potentially dangerous situation, anticipate the worst. Prepare yourself. But don't try to second guess what another driver will do. If you think the other driver will act a certain way, and he doesn't, you might react wrongly.

In a later chapter, we'll go into this topic of "other drivers" more deeply. But for now, let it suffice to say that the right mental attitude is far more important than you realize.

What's yours like?

Physical Conditioning

We've covered some of the mental aspects of riding a motorcycle; now let's see what's involved physically.

Expert motorcycling requires that your coordination, timing, and reflexes all function harmoniously to bring about that merging of motorcyclist and motorcycle.

Although bike riding in itself will help develop these faculties, you should have some program so you can further improve them. If you compete, especially motocross, you must be in good physical condition. Even if you remain a street rider, you need good timing and reflexes.

Any fast-moving activity like tennis, handball, speed-bag punching, or ping pong will sharpen your reflexes, timing, and coordination.

One of the simplist and most effective means for improving these faculties is by bouncing an ordinary ball against a wall and the ground and catching it. By throwing the ball at various angles, the eyes must quickly follow it. This exercise trains the eyes to constantly and rapidly shift from one point to another. When you've trained your eyes so they can shift quickly from point to point, take in a wider area to prevent staring, which will slow your reflexes. When you look at any point for more than three seconds, you become slower reacting.

Another good exercise for improving eyesight is to juggle two balls. It's important that you keep your eyes on the balls as they travel from one hand to the other. Your eyes must not "get ahead" of the balls. Because seeing is mostly a mental process (the mind has to interpret the images the eyes pick up), just making yourself more alert will improve vision somewhat.

If you ride extensively in the dirt and engage in motocross, enduro riding, or trials, you'll need to increase your endurance and strength in certain parts of your body. The arms, wrists, and hands must be strengthened to control the bike over rough terrain. For building strength in the legs and increasing endurance, jogging over rough terrain is excellent. Deep knee bends with weights are good, too. Also, don't overlook the value of strong stomach muscles to hold the vital organs in place as you bounce over rough terrain. Situps are effective here. For strengthening the hands and forearms, squeeze a rubber ball as hard as you can for at least a six-second count. Perform this exercise in ten- or fifteen-repetition cycles. This isometric exercise will give you a viselike grip, for hanging onto the handlebars in demanding off-road riding. Fingertip pushups are another good way to strengthen the hands and arms. If you're serious about staying fit, look into a program combining weight lifting, jogging, and swimming.

Here are a few tips for you serious off-road riders who need maximum endurance for grueling motocross or enduro riding. Shortly before an event, take a couple tablespoons of honey. It's absorbed immediately into the bloodstream and will increase your endurance. Wheat germ oil or vitamin E capsules should be a part of your daily diet.

If you fear broken bones from falling off your bike in a race, bone meal can be worth adding to your diet. Bone meal makes the bones stronger and more pliant so they can absorb more impact without fracturing or breaking.

Mental fitness and physical fitness complement each other. Don't overlook either in your quest to be an expert bike rider.

3
What You Should Wear

Because of your exposure to the elements and your vulnerability to possible injury from accidents, you must wear proper protective riding apparel.

If you're outfitted with the right protective clothing, you stand a good chance of walking away from most mishaps. If a cyclist can get free of his machine during a spill or impact with another vehicle, he has a good chance of survival.

Although it's commonly thought that a car motorist has a better chance of survival than a cyclist during an accident, it's not always true. Why? Well, the motorist who doesn't use his safety belt is thrown up against the windshield, steering wheel, roof, or the doors of his car during an impact. If the cyclist is properly dressed with helmet, eye protection, leather jacket, gloves, and boots, he has excellent protection from abrasion and impact with other objects.

The Safety Helmet

Because the safety helmet is generally regarded as a cyclist's most important piece of protection, let's take an in-depth look at helmets.

When purchasing a helmet, you must first decide what style you want.

There are three basic styles to choose from: the half-shell, the full-shell or jet type, and the total coverage or astronaut type.

For optimum protection and comfort, the full-shell is the most popular. It covers all the vital areas of the head, excluding the facial areas. The half-shell type is worn mostly by street riders who want a lightweight helmet for comfort. The total-coverage design offers the most protection. It's often chosen by racing enthusiasts, but it's bulky and hot in warm weather. However, it gives a boxed-in feeling that makes its wearer feel as though he's detached from his surroundings.

Some riders claim that the total-coverage style restricts lateral vision and reflects engine noise inside the shell.

Whichever style you choose, make sure it's a certified model. A moderately good helmet will be marked inside that it has passed the Z.90.1 standards. A reasonably good helmet will also have a sticker or label attached to the inside of its liner or shell with a statement such as, "This helmet meets or exceeds A.N.S.I. Z.90.1 safety standards." Look for it. Don't buy any helmet that doesn't have some label saying that it has passed certain testing standards.

The Snell standards are even more stringent than the one mentioned above. If your budget can afford it, buy a helmet that has met Snell specifications.

Safety helmets are made of fiberglass, high-impact plastic, or a combination of both materials. A disadvantage of plastic helmets is that their shells are susceptible to deterioration when exposed to solvents and chemicals. Whether you choose a fiberglass helmet or a high-impact plastic helmet, replace it every two or three years. The shell undergoes a molecular breakdown in its structure; the older it gets, the weaker the shell gets. If an older helmet should sustain a sharp impact, it'll tend to crack more quickly than would a new helmet.

Whenever you think of trying to save a few dollars on a cheap helmet, think what it would be like if your head struck an object during a mishap. Are you willing to chance that a cheap helmet can take the impact?

Once you've decided on the kind of helmet you want, next comes "fitting" your head to the right-size helmet. Don't ever buy a helmet without making sure it fits. If it doesn't fit, it can intensify an impact to your skull. An overly tight-fitting helmet will transmit more shock to the skull, instead of allowing the liner and shell to absorb most of the impact.

If the helmet fits loosely, it can tilt and expose the forehead. This condition is more liable to happen with a visor fitted, as the airstream can get under the visor and lift the helmet.

To check for proper helmet fit, put it on and fasten the chinstrap. Now push on the helmet from different angles; it shouldn't move around too much. Better to have it a little loose than too tight, though. If the liner is too hard and fits tightly, it'll cut off blood circulation and result in fatigue or even dizziness. A tight liner can impair hearing, too.

Once you've picked the right size helmet, look the shell over for defects. Check out the stitching in the chinstrap and the construction of the liner.

If it has a visor attached, make sure it's flexible enough to fold under (or pop off, if it's held by fasteners) so it won't snag on anything in the event of a spill.

Get a *good* helmet and take *good* care of it.

Eye Protection

Complementing the safety helmet is some form of eye protection. And considering the sensitive nature of the eyes and their vulnerability to air pressure, dirt, and flying objects, they, too, deserve the very best in protection.

Let's see how you can provide it.

For street riding
minimum protective
riding gear should
include a certified
helmet, properly
fastened, and snug-
fitting eyewear.
*(Courtesy Kawasaki
Motor Corp.)*

You can choose from goggles, riding glasses, and face shields. Because windshields or fairings don't provide maximum protection, we'll omit them here.

There are many styles of goggles from which to choose. Plastic-lens types are the most popular, but they scratch easily, as compared with glass lenses. The better-grade goggles are made of scratch-resistant polycarbonate lenses.

The most appealing feature of goggles is that they provide a tighter fit around the eyes than other forms of eye wear and keep out dirt and air turbulence.

When purchasing plastic-lens goggles, hold them up to a light at arms length. Then slowly move them around to check for any distortion in the plastic. Cheaper-made goggles are particularly prone to optical defects. Such goggles can cause visual impairment, headaches, and nausea.

Since plastic lenses scratch easily, you must treat them with care. Never use an abrasive cloth or paper towel to clean them. When not in use, store them where they won't be knocked about and exposed to dirt, dust, and solvents.

Badly scratched lenses are particularly annoying at night when they refract oncoming headlight beams. Add fog or rain to those headlight beams, and you can understand how vision would be affected.

The advantage of plastic-lens goggles is that they're inexpensive to replace, providing you don't have to do it often. And you can keep different shades of lenses on hand, since most plastic-lens goggles feature interchangeable lenses. That's the disadvantage of glass-lens goggles: their lenses aren't usually replaceable, although they won't scratch easily. But if you get glass lenses, make sure they're tempered to resist breakage.

As for the color of lenses, whether they're plastic or glass, clear lenses are recommended for night and low-light day-riding conditions. For sunny conditions, use either a smoked (gray) or a green tint, because these colors will filter out harmful ultraviolet and infrared rays and still provide good color definition. The latter is important for distinguishing traffic signals and warning lights. Stay away from blue lenses. They distort visible light and allow ultraviolet and infrared rays to pass through. Amber lenses are okay for dusk or hazy conditions, but they distort green and yellow traffic lights.

Goggles should fit snugly without putting pressure on the sinus areas. Any gaps around the nose areas will permit easy entry for an airstream into the eyes.

Check also for lateral vision. There should be no obstruction of side vision from the frame. Another good idea is to make sure the goggles are vented to keep moisture from building up on the inside of the lens. Spend a little more and get the type of polycarbonate lens that absorbs moisture in damp weather, preventing fogging.

If you wear glasses, you might consider having your glass goggles fitted with prescription lenses. They're well worth the extra cost for their convenience and comfort.

For moderate-speed riding, you might consider riding glasses or sunglasses. Riding glasses feature large lenses and hinged nose pieces that allow the lenses to conform to the curvature of the face and nose, thereby minimizing the airstream into the eyes. Usually constructed of tempered glass, riding glasses have wire ear pieces so they won't be dislodged easily. Sunglasses are least effective for eye protection. Their fixed nose pieces don't allow them to conform to the curvature of the face. They usually have smaller lenses that don't offer much protection. And unless you buy a good glass-lens type, sunglasses of the dime-store/drug-store variety often have optical imperfections.

For low-speed, in-town riding, you can get by with sunglasses. Discard them, though, when you get out on the highways.

For maximum facial coverage and eye protection, faceshields are the way to go. There are different styles available, ranging from full-facial types that are bubble-shaped to halfshields that cover only the upper portion of the face. A big plus for the faceshield is that it keeps rain from stinging your face. In dry weather, it keeps bugs out.

Faceshields do interfere with that feeling of being out in the open, however. But for extended touring, especially in the rain, a faceshield is ideal. Buy the type that has a special chemical coating to absorb moisture and prevent fogging.

There are some drawbacks to the faceshield. A layer of dirt or dust can deposit itself on the shield under dusty off-road conditions. And reflection of engine noise can be annoying to some riders. Like plastic goggles, scratching is a problem.

Each form of eye protection has its advantages and disadvantages. You must decide which is best for you.

What about Clothing

Despite the emphasis on head and eye protection, the rest of your body needs looking after, too.

Whether it's the upper body, legs, hands, or feet, the best protection is leather. It offers warmth, protection against abrasion, suppleness, durability, water repellency (when treated), and comfort. Besides leather, protective clothing is also available in vinyl.

Competitive motorcycling events require heavy footwear and leathers, not to mention a good helmet and eye protection. *(Courtesy Yamaha International Corp.)*

Warmth and water-repellency are vinyl's biggest advantages. But it doesn't have the scuff resistance of leather. Nylon ski jackets also make excellent apparel for warmth without weight and excessive bulk. Surprisingly, nylon has good scuff resistance, as its "slipperiness" prevents it from snagging during a spill.

In fact, whatever material your jacket is made of, make sure it has a slippery lining, like nylon or satin. Reason? In the event of a spill, the lining will keep you from sustaining brush burn as you slide around inside the jacket. Same goes for any leather or vinyl riding pants you wear over regular pants.

Now let's see what a good cycling jacket should feature.

Like a helmet and eye protection, a jacket must fit well. It should be snug, not loose, not tight. The idea is to keep it against the body to retain body heat without hindering movement. The sleeves should have either zipper or elasticized enclosures to keep air from seeping up your sleeves. And make sure the jacket is long enough in back so that the airstream can't sneak up your backside.

Another advantage of a regular motorcycle jacket or ski jacket is that it will have some form of waist enclosure to keep the air out.

Another point to check for in a jacket is the collar. It shouldn't flutter in the airstream too much. Also make sure that with the front zipper in the top-most position, air can't funnel down your neck. Of course, you can always wear a scarf.

So much for jackets. What about pants?

Virtually any heavy material like denim will do the job. If you ride any lengthy distance with lightweight pants, they might flap around and chafe your legs.

For cold weather, you might try leather or vinyl pants.

When getting fitted for a pair of riding pants or a snowmobiling-type suit, make sure the pants are long enough when you're in a riding position. You don't want cold air

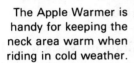

The Apple Warmer is handy for keeping the neck area warm when riding in cold weather.

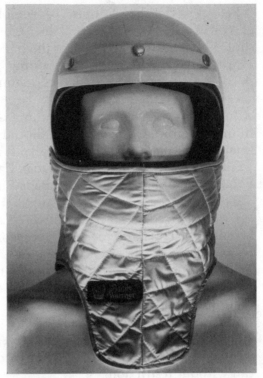

finding its way up your legs. For warm-weather riding, lightweight coveralls are ideal for keeping your street clothes clean. Although it might appear gaudy, choose bright clothing. You'll be more noticeable to other drivers.

Now let's look at the extremities, the hands and feet.

Gloves not only keep your hands warm in cold weather, they also allow better grasping of the handlebar grips and provide protection against abrasion, if a spill occurs.

For warm weather, perforated gloves are effective for preventing excessive perspiration while not reducing protection that much. Warm-weather gloves can be made by punching holes in a pair of cheaper buckskin gloves and by cutting off the fingertips.

Because your hands must be flexible, use thermally lined gloves in cold weather. Don't buy gloves too small, or they'll shut off circulation and permit the hands to get cold faster.

Mitts aren't practical for bike riding, not enough flexibility.

To keep air out of your sleeves, gauntlets are worthwhile.

Footwear. Which is best?

Just think, your feet are skimming along only a few inches from the ground. If your foot should happen to slip off the footrest, or you happen to have a spill and slide for a distance, would you want to be wearing light, low-cut footwear? Footwear should be at least six inches high, preferably higher.

The idea is to protect the ankle. Higher footwear is less easily dislodged, if it's a good fit. Lace-up boots are ideal, because they're hard to come loose during a mishap. High boots that have zipper enclosures are the next best choice. For motocross or trials, specialized footwear is recommended.

For maximum protection, get boots or shoes with steel toes, high heels, and thick soles.

For the dirt rider, especially the motocrosser, there are specialized protective items like faceguards, elbow guards, chest and shoulder pads, etc. Wear as much protection as you can without restriction.

If you're a street rider, at least wear the basic items described in this chapter.

And remember, buy the very best, *for your sake.*

4
What You Should Know about Motorcycles

Now you're going to look at another vital aspect of expert motorcycling: how a motorcycle performs and steers. To expertly operate a motorcycle, you must come to know how it behaves or handles under a variety of conditions. Obviously it takes lots of conscientious riding to "feel out" a motorcycle.

But in your quest to master the motorcycle, you should combine some theory with your saddle time. In other words, you should have some knowledge of the basic principles that govern a motorcycle's behavior.

When you understand the reasons behind a motorcycle's behavior, you can operate it more intelligently. You then have a good idea of what to expect during certain maneuvers and can react accordingly.

What Keeps the Bike Upright?

Like a bicycle, a motorcycle depends on forward motion to generate stability.

And what makes the motorcycle so amazingly stable when moving is the gyroscopic inertia of its spinning wheels. What that means is the two wheels are functioning like gyroscopes. And if you've ever played with a rapidly spinning toy gyro or top, you'll recall how it resisted any force that attempted to topple it.

Whether it's the tiniest toy gyro or the largest motorcycle, the same gyro-stabilization principle applies to both.

But unlike the toy gyro, which has only its own mass to contend with, the wheels of a motorcycle must hold up many times their own weight. But thanks to gyroscopic inertia, they do it.

Without precession, the motorcycle wouldn't have such uncanny self-stabilization. Precession occurs when a disturbing force is applied at a right angle to the wheel's spin axis or axle. The wheel turns, or precesses, toward the disturbing force. Precession is the self-stabilizing tendency of a wheel to "shake off" any force that attempts to divert it from its course. Were it not for its capacity to precess when disturbed, a spinning body would be very unstable.

The following illustration shows how the front wheel changes direction according to the angle in which a force is applied to the spin axis.

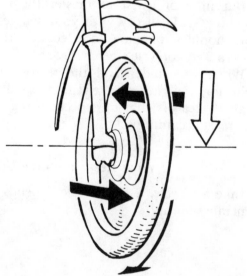

The front wheel changes
direction according
to the angle in which
a force is applied
to the spin axis.

If a downward force should be exerted against one end of the spin axis, the wheel would turn or swivel around its vertical axis toward that side from which the disturbing force would be applied. Now, if a force were applied to one end of the spin axis, in a direction parallel to the ground, the wheel would tilt instead of swivel toward the disturbing force.

You can prove this last form of precession to yourself by getting your bike airborne, then turning the handlebar to one side. You might become alarmed, though, when you find the bike leaning to the opposite side in which the handlebar was turned. Besides, you could end up in a nasty spill. So just accept the fact that precession does act in such ways.

The rear wheel tries to precess, too, but it's held in check by the frame.

Despite the wheels' gyroscopic properties, there is something else that contributes to your bike's amazing self-stabilizing behavior—tires. If tires didn't distort under load, even gyroscopic inertia and precession wouldn't be able to keep a two-wheeler upright all the time.

You see, whenever the front wheel turns slightly to one side when moving, the tire distorts at its contact point and twists itself back into line again, until the front wheel is again tracking straight ahead.

But if the front wheel violently deflects to one side or becomes airborne and lands at an angle opposite its previous direction, it will build up enough momentum to snap back, past center, and over to the other side. The wheel will swivel, or oscillate back and forth until its momentum diminishes and it's tracking straight ahead again. In most cases, this "pendulum" action isn't noticeable. But whenever the wheel swings from side to side, it induces precessional forces.

Furthermore, if the precessional forces should act in harmony with the oscillating action of the wheel and fork assembly, a violent fork wobble may occur. When this happens, each time the wheel swings to one side, the energy of the oscillating wheel increases until the fork is banging against the fork stops. That is, the fork is swinging as far as it can to either side.

Although fork wobble is rare today with well-designed motorcycles, it can be initiated by altering the bike's steering geometry.

Odd-size tires, modified frame and fork, even loose or worn steering-head bearings, can cause some degree of fork wobble. Besides improved frame design and construction, improved tire technology is a major reason for minimal fork wobble on modern bikes. Modern tires are more stable than their predecessors. With their more-rigid internal construction, today's tires don't flex excessively so as to induce fork wobble.

But mounting a heavier tire than specified by the motorcycle manufacturer can cause significant increase in the tire's gyroscopic behavior and self-alignment tendency.

Camber thrust is a term that describes another characteristic of the pneumatic tire. When the bike is tracking straight ahead and hits a bump, camber thrust stabilizes the tire by pulling it up the side of the bump. And whenever the tire is angled to the ground surface, camber thrust pushes the tire back upright.

So, with forces like gyroscopic inertia, precession, self-alignment torque, camber thrust, even centrifugal force, a motorcycle can practically steer itself. In fact, if the bike is moving fast enough, the handlebars are nothing more than a resting place for the hands.

But at very low speeds, where there is little gyroscopic inertia to keep the two-wheeler upright, and it's weaving to stay balanced, the handlebars do become a steering control.

How the Motorcycle Corners

One of the mysterious aspects of a motorcycle's steering behavior is its ability to corner.

Here the motorcycle takes on a new dimension of movement, much like that of an airplane, as it banks for a turn. Of course, the cycle's up and down movement when banked is considerably less than that of a turning airplane. But the bike's closeness to the ground gives you a sensation of movement and speed that the pilot of an airplane doesn't experience.

Anyway, just what does happen to make a motorcycle corner?

It comes right back to gyroscopic precession. When you desire to turn in a particular direction, you either lean to that direction, or exert some force against the bike to "push" it over.

By "pushing" or leaning the bike over, you apply a disturbing force to the end of the front wheel spin axis. The wheel then precesses in that direction in an attempt to stabilize the

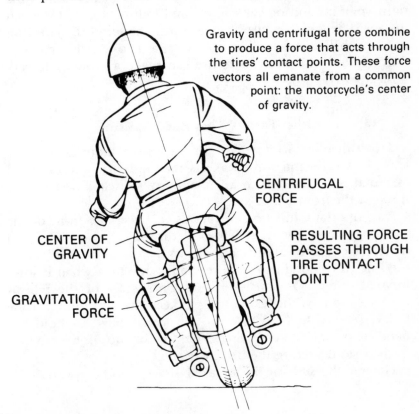

Gravity and centrifugal force combine to produce a force that acts through the tires' contact points. These force vectors all emanate from a common point: the motorcycle's center of gravity.

CENTRIFUGAL FORCE

CENTER OF GRAVITY

RESULTING FORCE PASSES THROUGH TIRE CONTACT POINT

GRAVITATIONAL FORCE

bike. Exerting force on any part of the motorcycle, like the handlebar, side of the gas tank, or top of the footrest, will make the front wheel precess.

Tire distortion enters the picture again, too. When the bike is banked over, the tire distorts at its contact point to produce a condition known as slip angle. What this means is that the wheel is pointing in one direction, and the tire is traveling in another direction. The road or ground surface pushes against the tire, making it travel more toward the outside of the turn.

Slip angle is a safety factor for the bike rider. For it automatically corrects somewhat for sharp cornering. The more the tire distorts under hard cornering/sharp bank angles, the more pronounced the slip angle, the wider the turn.

A well-designed motorcycle will automatically select the right combination of bank angle and radius of turn to match the speed at which a turn is taken. Just changing tire sizes can make a big difference in the way a two-wheeler corners. Furthermore, the wrong size tire can make a motorcycle very unsteady in a turn.

Other Factors That Effect Steering

Two other factors involved in the way a motorcycle steers are called rake and trail. Rake is the angle the steering-head axis makes in relation to an imaginary vertical line running through the front-wheel axle.

An important function of rake is to lower the front of the machine when the handlebar is turned to one side. If a motorcycle has the right amount of rake, its front will lean to the side just enough to help restabilize the bike when it loses forward speed. Obviously, if the gyro effect of the wheels becomes too low, there's nothing to keep the bike going. If the fork assembly had no rake at all, you'd have to hold the handlebars rigidly at all times, for fear of the slightest bump in the road deflecting the front wheel.

Having the steering head raked serves another purpose. It

keeps handlebar length within reason. If there were no rake at all, the handlebar would have to be so long that it would produce a tillerlike effect. The danger from such a setup would be that the slightest movement of the handlebars would induce too much steering-leverage effect.

Working with rake is a dimension called trail. It's the self-centering action of the front wheel (not to be confused with the tire's self-alignment caused by distortion).

Rake and trail must be adjusted properly to prevent steering problems.

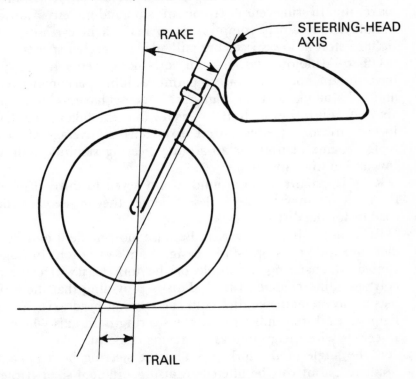

A good example of trail is to be found in the casters used on furniture. Whenever a caster-wheeled item is put into motion, the wheels swing around until they're rolling in the direction they're being pushed. Trail is the distance the tire's contact point "trails" behind the steering-head-axis/point-of-ground intersection.

The amount of trail is critical for determining whether a motorcycle will have light or heavy steering. The designer of a motorcycle tries to incorporate the right amount of trail and rake to complement the machine's wheelbase for ensuring good steering. A small amount of trail will make the steering light at low speeds. But at high speeds, it will make the front end seem light and unstable. A considerable amount of trail will give a motorcycle stability at high speeds, but it will also make the steering cumbersome in stop-and-go city riding. Motorcycle designers compromise to make a bike reasonably light to steer at low speeds but still stable at higher speeds.

Off-road motorcycles used in low-speed events like trails have small amounts of trail to permit walking-pace maneuverability. Mounts used for high-speed racing have as much as six or seven inches of trail to ensure that the bikes have that locked-on-course feeling. Street bikes have an average of four to five inches of trail for all-around steering stability both at low and at high speeds.

Rake is usually set at around twenty-seven to thirty degrees for most motorcycles, regardless whether they're used for the road or for the dirt.

Rake and trail can be varied. Because most modern motorcycles use the telescopic-fork design, any variation in rake caused by changing the angle of the fork legs will cause a corresponding change in trail. This is providing that the fork legs always remain parallel with the steering-head axis. When figuring trail, remember to use the steering-head axis where it intersects with the ground as the reference point.

If the angle of the fork legs and the steering head remain unaltered, trail can be altered by using different-sized triple-fork crowns. They attach the fork legs to the stem that runs through the steering head. Some riders use a rake plate (an upper triple clamp that pulls the tops of the fork legs back toward the steering head) to stretch the wheelbase.

A rake plate reduces trail. And if the fork legs are pulled out of parallel with the steering head axis by more than a couple of degrees, handling is negatively effected.

Wheelbase can be altered by lengthening the rear swing arm by using different-size triple clamps, like the rake plate, and by having a section cut away from the top of the frame behind the steering head. The two sections of the top frame member are then welded together. Chopper builders use this method a lot to extend the front end.

Another method used to extend the front end is to employ fork-leg extensions that make the bike sit higher off the ground. As long as the fork legs remain parallel with the head axis, trail is increased when fork-leg extensions are added. But excessively long fork legs can make for considerable leverage from road shock. This places more stress on the frame.

Although extended fork legs look racy, they make for sluggish handling at low speeds and increase the turning radius.

Another modification to be careful of is the mounting of odd-size tires. Whenever odd-size tires are mounted, they change rake and trail dimensions. For instance, if you put a larger wheel on the front, the front end becomes elevated, thereby increasing both rake and trail. If you mount a larger tire on the back, you increase the distance that the bike sits off the ground in the rear and consequently steepen the fork angle up front. Should you put larger but equally sized tires on both front and back, you raise the bike off the ground more and lengthen the trail dimension.

Regardless how you juggle wheel sizes around, the wheelbase won't change, because it's determined by measuring from axle center to axle center.

When it comes to modifying your bike, make sure the modification doesn't adversely effect the bike's handling ability. Don't modify your motorcycle just for style. If a modification contributes to improved handling, fine. If not, forget it.

Whether it's a change in the handlebar design, suspension,

tires, or even the viscosity of the oil in the fork legs, realize that there'll be some effect on the handling.

Because you want to become an expert rider, you must have a good-handling bike. The two of you must become a smoothly functioning unit. If your bike has some handling peculiarities, correct them. If you must alter anything, do so intelligently.

You have only two wheels; you can't afford to take chances with them.

5

How to Set Up Your Bike

There's something intriguing about the way an expert rider handles his bike.

Whether he's laying it over for a turn or just going through the gears, he performs smoothly. He seems a part of his two-wheeler.

If you've yet to reach that state of "oneness" with your bike, you must realize that your bike is essentially an extension of *you*. And any movement by you is instantly transmitted to that machine. Furthermore, its single-track nature is far more sensitive than any car.

It's this sensitivity that makes the correct seating position and placement of controls critical. To control your bike, you must feel "right" with it.

Many cyclists never really set up their bikes for better control and comfort. Instead of modifying the seating/controls layout to their own requirements, they conform to their bikes. As a result, they never gain the comfort and control that is possible.

Any improvement you make to your bike so that you come that much closer to total control is what we're after. That's the goal of the expert—total control.

First, you must establish the proper handlebar/seat/footrest relationship. To do so, make sure your bike is sitting in a normal upright position.

The Handlebar Assembly

Because of the differences in arm reach, posture, etc., few riders are matched to stock handlebars. Even though the handlebar, when the bike's moving fast enough, is nothing more than a resting place for the hands, it's still a control.

The wrong handlebar will reveal itself during a long ride or when maneuvering at low speeds.

The correct handlebar depends on its height and angles of the bends throughout its length. For most street riding, a moderately high bar (two to eight inches) is recommended.

A certain amount of sweepback is desirable to keep you from having to bend too far forward.

But if you're a racer, you want the low, clip-on design that allows you to crouch. For normal road riding, however, a clip-on bar can become very tiring. To the other extreme, we have the high-riser or "ape" bar. The trouble with this design is that it can induce too much steering leverage, resulting in overcontrol. Between these two extremes of clip-on and high-riser, you'll find a wide variety of handlebar designs to suit your tastes.

When choosing a handlebar, make sure that your wrists and hands don't have to bend at uncomfortable angles when operating the controls.

The only practical way to determine the right handlebar is to try one for a while. If the stock handlebar isn't too uncomfortable, chances are you'll adapt to it. Most riders do.

Okay, now let's see how to adjust the handlebar. To adjust the bar for height, sit on your bike with it on the level, close your eyes, and reach out to where your arms and hands feel comfortable. Then open your eyes. Notice where the grips are in relation to your hands. You may have to raise or lower the bar a few inches for comfort.

If you don't want to change the handlebar design but want to relocate the bar forward or backward, or alter its height, look into a riser kit. They are extensions that attach the bar to a mini handlebar located in the stock handlebar mounting.

Some riders will rubber-mount their handlebars so that a minimum of vibration and shock is transmitted to their upper body. But rubber-mounted bars interfere with that close feeling a rider should have with his bike.

Don't overlook the matter of choosing the right handgrips, either. They should be large enough to permit a good grip, yet not so large that the hands must squeeze hard to keep hold

With the handlebar at the right height, position the front brake and clutch levers so that the wrists don't have to bend awkwardly to operate them.

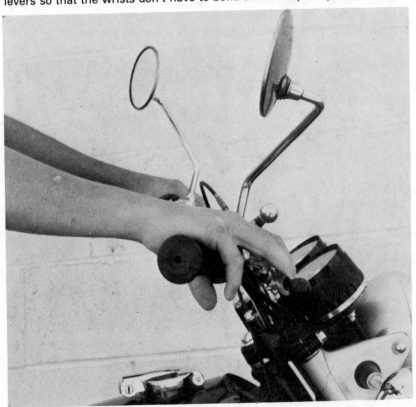

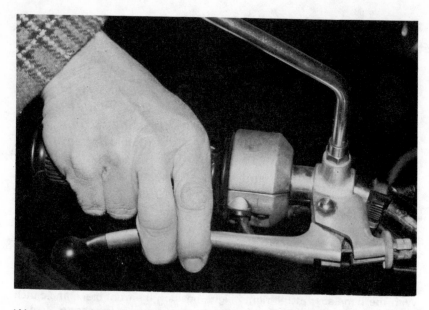

(Above) Set up the front brake so its lever is easily operable with two-finger pressure. (Below) Auxiliary controls, like the compression release shown here, should be located where they are easily reached.

of them. However, if the grips are too narrow, the hands can't clench them effectively, because the fingers will dig into the palms.

The grips must be soft enough to prevent the hands from becoming sore; yet, they must be firm to ensure gripping. A too-soft grip will quickly tire the hand, because you'll have to exert too much force to hold it.

The grips should have some type of projections on their surfaces to provide adequate "traction." If the grips are smooth, some form of abrasive substance may be cemented to them. Another alternative is to cut grooves or slits into the grips.

Once you've situated the handlebar the way you want it, next comes the positioning of the clutch and front-brake levers.

Sitting on the bike with the hands resting on the grips, the hands and forearms should be in line when the levers are operated. In other words, when a lever is squeezed, the hand or wrist shouldn't have to bend awkwardly.

To reposition the levers, simply slacken their securing clamps and slowly turn them around the handlebar until they're in line with your arms, wrists, and hands.

Once you've positioned the levers, adjust their cables for play. Cable adjustments can usually be done with the knurled adjusters located on the cable housings where they enter into the lever assemblies.

The clutch cable must have slack before the clutch plates disengage, or the plates won't press firmly against one another when the clutch is engaged. When the lever is squeezed hard enough to disengage the clutch plates, about one-eighth inch of cable should be exposed near its attachment to the hand lever. It there's too much slack in the clutch cable, the plates won't separate far enough when the lever is squeezed. The results will be clutch drag and grinding gear shifts.

The front-brake cable should have enough slack in it so that the hand lever moves about one-third of the way before the brake engages. The reason for this is that the fingers can squeeze harder once they're partially clenched. Just be sure that the lever doesn't hit against the handlebar when it's squeezed hard.

If you have to squeeze the brake lever hard to operate the brake, you might want to put on a longer hand lever for more leverage. Some riders even mount extensions on the brake-cam levers. This latter technique does, of course, not apply to disc-type brakes.

Another technique for applying the front brake more effectively is to position the fingers out more toward the end of the lever. Hopefully, you'll have a ball-ended lever so the fingers don't slip off.

Actually, the front brake should be operable with one- or two-finger pressure.

After you've adjusted the hand levers for cable slack, check them for sideplay. They shouldn't flop around, yet they mustn't be so tight that they bind when squeezed.

The throttle cable shouldn't bind when the throttle is moved. Most throttles snap back when they're released.

As for the horn, headlight dimmer, turn signal lever, etc., they should all be accessible without having to remove your hands from the grips.

Don't overlook mirror placement. You should have at least one mirror, located on the left side of the handlebar. Factory mirrors usually don't have much adjustment allowable. If you can't place such mirrors satisfactorily, take them off and mount the type that clamp to the handlebar.

When adjusting mirrors, again make sure the bike is level. Also, make sure you can see rearward with a passenger in position.

As for the lens, a wide-diameter, flat lens is desirable, because it provides a distortion-free image. The convex lens, so popular on factory-equipped bikes, takes in a greater area, but it also yields a false sense of distance between your machine and a vehicle behind you. If you employ a convex-type lens, always check over your shoulder before pulling out to pass someone.

In fact, regardless of what type of mirror you use and how many you have, never pull out from a curb or into another lane without looking over your shoulder. More on that later.

Seating Position

Most motorcycles have no provision for adjusting the seat. About the only significant alternative is to replace the stock seat with one that is more suitable for your posterior. Since road-going bikes have their seat heights about thirty-one to thirty-three inches from the ground, anyone under 5'10'' has trouble putting his feet on the ground.

Bikes with eighteen-inch wheels cater more to the smaller rider. So if you're fairly short, shy away from anything with a twenty-one-inch front wheel.

A seat shouldn't be so wide that the thighs have to splay away from the gas tank. You want as much of your body in contact with the bike as possible. If you find the seat too hard, put on a padded seat cover or take the original cover off and place a sheet of foam underneath.

If you always ride solo, you can gain a lower, often more comfortable seating position by going to a specially made solo saddle.

The proper seating position, where the primary controls fall readily to hand and foot, will enable you to have effective control of your bike.

Footrests

Footrests help establish a good seating position. They're steering controls in a sense. By exerting body weight to either footrest, you can make the bike change direction. Some motorcycles have adjustable footrests, allowing for precise location of the feet.

Street bikes have their footrests placed farther forward than dirt bikes. The footrests shouldn't be too far forward, however, because it's difficult to rise on them or "post" when the bike strikes potholes and other shock producers. Because a dirt rider spends more time up on the pegs than a street jockey, his footrests should be situated more to the rear for better control. If you ride both dirt and street, compromise.

For normal riding, you should have the footrests placed so that they're located slightly ahead of your seating position. The lower legs shouldn't have to bend uncomfortably, or else the footrests are too far rearward and possibly too high.

If your footrests are adjustable, experiment with different positions until they feel comfortable and still enable you to post without feeling awkward or losing your balance.

After you've situated the footrests, you can then reposition the rear-brake pedal and gearshift lever.

Relocate the brake arm to where the pedal lies about one-fourth to one-half inch below the sole of the foot, with your foot resting in a natural position. Make sure that your foot won't apply the brake, unless intended. Having the pedal too close to the foot will result in your foot "riding" the brake.

Because the gearshift lever is usually mounted on a serrated shaft, it's a simple matter of taking it off and repositioning it so that it can be operated without having to move the toe very far. If you have to lift either foot off the footrest to operate its respective control, you lose unity with your bike, plus you cut down on your capacity to react quickly.

Other Adjustments

There are other ways of setting up your bike to make it more responsive and safe to ride.

Take the suspension units, for example. Depending on whether you want a soft or a firm ride, you can put different springs in the fork legs and change the rear shocks. Even changing the viscosity of the oil used in the fork legs will alter the damping characteristics.

Rear shocks usually have different settings on the bigger bikes so that a firmer or a softer ride can be "dialed" in.

Don't overlook seemingly minor points like tire pressure, either.

Some older, large-capacity bikes have steering dampers fitted to vary the side-to-side movement of the fork assembly. If the damper is too tight, it'll make the steering awkward at low speeds.

Set up your bike so that every control can be operated with minimum effort. The idea is to blend into your bike. You may have to experiment with different control positions, but it's worth it.

6

Is Your Bike Safe to Ride?

You must keep your steed in top-running condition. After all, you don't have the margin for error that the four-wheel driver has. If you blow a tire or break a chain, it could be disastrous.

Furthermore, the mechanical nature of the motorcycle makes periodic maintenance a *must*. One reason is that modern bikes are operated at much higher engine speeds and perform under greater stress than most multi-wheeled vehicles. Therefore, they need more looking after. Because vibration is an inherent problem of most motorcycles, components can loosen frequently. Road shock also contributes to vibration.

How much maintenance a motorcycle needs depends a lot on the construction of the bike and on the way it's ridden. Obviously if a high-performance machine is ridden hard constantly, it'll need more looking after than one that is ridden infrequently and conservatively. You're the one who must decide what has to be done and how often.

Now, if you're a person who can't tell a sparkplug from a spoke, you might become irritated at the amount of maintenance needed to keep a motorcycle running. But once you come to know what has to be done and how to do it, you come to enjoy keeping your bike up to snuff.

What's more, if you keep after your bike regularly, using preventive-maintenance, you'll keep your bike's problems from becoming serious.

The Professional Approach

You'll find there's always something more to learn. To increase your storehouse of knowledge and mechanical skills, take advantage of the written word.

Dozens of motorcycle magazines offer timely and informative articles on maintenance, tuning, and modification. Plus there are numerous books available that cover virtually every facet of motorcycling. One publication you should definitely add to your motorcycling library is a comprehensive service and overhaul manual, if you plan to get into serious maintenance.

Clip out pertinent articles on motorcycle maintenance and keep them in a loose-leaf notebook. Refer to them when your bike has a problem.

Don't be afraid to ask questions; just ask the right people.

Let's say that you're reasonably new to motorcycles. Yet, you want to learn how to do basic maintenance yourself. What do you do? The best way to learn how to do something is to first learn to master the simpler things. You can start off with something simple like adjusting the rear chain or the control cables. Then you can move on to setting the valves and the carburetor; setting the ignition timing might be your next goal. As your skills increase, you might undertake a top-end overhaul. In time, you might complete overhauls and engine modifications.

Always make sure you thoroughly understand each step.

Before you perform anything, study the service manual. Don't take something apart just for the sake of it; work on your bike intelligently.

Keep records of all major maintenance performed—tune-ups, oil changes, gearing changes, etc. You can hang a chart in your garage or workshop, or keep a notebook in your toolbox. By keeping records you always have an accurate means to determine what has been done.

Another good idea is to make a written checklist of your bike for periodic-maintenance inspections.

The purpose of a checklist is that it prompts you to cover your bike thoroughly in an organized manner. Items to be inspected should be written down in a systematic order. As each item is checked and, if need be, worked on, check it off and make a notation alongside the checkmark. If you don't use a checklist, you'll tend to overlook components at times.

You actually save time with a checklist, too, because you always follow the same sequence. And by making notations of what has to be done, you always have a means of checking back to see what has been done during past inspections. For example, if you find a certain bolt loose, and your records show that it has loosened before, you know that it needs particular attention to keep it from recurring.

When making your checklist, divide the bike into sections. For instance, the front wheel and fork assembly can be considered a unit; the handlebar and its controls can be another unit. The engine area can comprise a unit in itself, with the rear-wheel and swing-arm assemblies making another unit. The lights and electrical system can be listed as a separate unit or included with other sections.

Regardless how you do it, the important thing is that the various components are listed. You don't need to list every nut and bolt; rather, you can list groups of items like engine bolts or nuts.

Once you find a workable system, stick to it.

To give you an idea of what to check for, we're going

to conduct a combination safety-inspection/maintenance-program.

You're not going to go over your bike with a fine tooth comb every time you want to take a spin. But certain components—tires, chains and sprockets, control cables, lights, and brakes—should come under frequent scrutiny.

Keep Your Bike Clean

If you take pride in your bike, you'll never let it become encrusted with dirt and grease. A clean machine not only reflects pride of ownership, but makes it easier to spot something wrong. And there's something about a dirt-free bike that stimulates the owner to keep it in top-notch condition.

The Front Wheel

What more logical place to start our inspection-maintenance program.

Before we begin, you have, of course, the bike's tool kit and other necessary tools close by, along with the bike's owner's manual, right? Hopefully, you've nearly memorized the owner's manual. If not, make friends with it. The owner's manual isn't as comprehensive as a service manual, but it's sufficient for checking out the basics.

Let's start off by examining the tire for small stones and other objects that may have become imbedded in the tread. Look for small tears or bruises in the sidewalls that may lead to tire failure later. One of the simplest and most important steps you can undertake in bike care is checking the tire pressure. A good-quality air-pressure gauge is one of the most important tools you can own.

When you think that your mount pivots on two small patches of rubber and that the tire pressure has a major effect on how well those patches grip the ground, then it's foolhardy to neglect checking tire pressure. You see, not only does air pressure have a lot to do with how well a tire performs, but it also determines how long it can last.

For example, a tire that runs at eighty percent of its normal pressure will lose as much as thirty percent of its life. A soft tire wears away more side tread when cornering. When too much side tread is worn away, your chances for skidding on a turn increase. A too-soft tire also makes for squirrelly handling when tracking straight ahead.

An underinflated tire will flex more, thereby building up excessive heat through internal friction that can lead to failure of the tire casing. Also, a soft tire will absorb more power from the engine, which will produce poor performance and lower gas mileage. However, you can run a tire two or three pounds under recommended pressures given in the owner's manual without ill effects.

Overinflation has its drawbacks, too. If a tire has too much air pressure, it can lead to skidding, instability, reduced stopping distance, and premature wear of the tire's center-tread area. Moreover, an overinflated tire is more likely to suffer damage from impact with rocks, curbs, pot holes, and sharp objects.

Actually, it's better to have tires slightly overinflated than underinflated. Going above recommended pressures by fifteen to twenty percent will slightly increase mileage and performance. And don't overlook the fact that stopping distance will be slightly reduced.

Tire pressure should be checked at least once a week; twice a week if you ride a lot. If you're on a cross-country trip, running several hours or more at a clip, check pressure daily.

Play it safe and go by what the owner's manual and tire manufacturer recommend. Don't ever run on a flat tire, or the distortion of the sidewalls will separate the cords in the casing. Make sure the valve has a tightly fitted cap. Don't park your bike where the tires will be exposed to grease, oil, or other solvents. Wipe such deposits off with a gasoline-soaked rag.

Be careful when riding with new tires. They are slippery until they've had a chance to wear away some of their surface.

Oftentimes a front tire will wear unevenly. Reversing the tire's direction of rotation by remounting can increase the life of the tire. If you find the front tire wearing irregularly, it may also be evidence of an unbalanced tire, especially if it's new. It's easy to static balance a tire. With the wheel elevated so the tire is free to rotate, make a chalk mark on the tire and set it spinning. Note where the chalk mark comes to rest. After a few such spins/stops, if the chalk mark always stops in the same place, the tire is out of balance.

Then it's a matter of placing different-weight wheel weights or pieces of solder diametrically opposite the tire's "heavy" spot, until the tire stops at different locations when it's rotated. An alternative to messing with weights is to inject a pressurized can of TBF (tire balance fluid) directly into the inner tube. Many riders swear by it.

Whichever method you use, you'll find that a balanced tire will make your bike run smoother and stabler.

So much for the tire.

How about the spokes? To determine if they're loose, strike each with a wrench. A tight spoke will emit a "ping," while a loose spoke will have a dull sound. Another method to check tension is to squeeze two spokes together.

Are the nuts tight that hold the axle in place? How about the fender braces? If a drum brake is used, make sure the cable attachment is secure. If a disc brake is fitted, see that no hydraulic fluid is leaking. The puck or pad may have a marking on it to indicate the amount of wear left. Check it.

Do the fork seals leak? They shouldn't!

To check for worn or loose steering-head bearings, and/or worn fork-leg bushings, elevate the front wheel and squat down in front of the bike. Grasp both fork legs and rock them frontward and backward. There shouldn't be any perceptible play.

It's just as bad to have steering-head bearings that are too

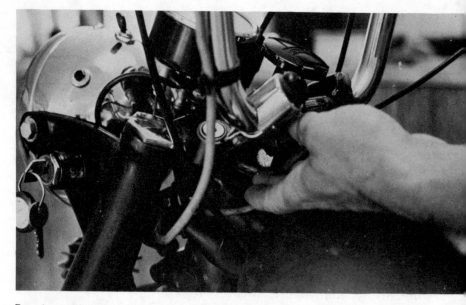

For detecting wear in steering-head bearings, place fingertips between cap and steering head, while rocking bike back and forth with front brake applied.

tight. With the wheel still elevated, slowly swing the fork from side to side. There shouldn't be any sticking or binding.

The Handlebar Assembly

There's another way you can check for loose steering-head bearings—from behind the handlebar. Apply the front brake, and with the fingertips of the left hand placed over the gap between the steering head and the bearing cap, rock the bike. If there's any play, you'll feel it.

Shake the handlebar. It shouldn't move. Take a wrench or a screwdriver and check the front-brake and clutch-lever clamps that hold them to the handlebar. Squeeze the levers and see if the cables need lubricating. Cable lubricating is made easier with injector-type lubricators. Keep all the cables well lubricated—clutch, front-brake, and throttle. While you're looking at the cables, do you notice any frayed strands? If only one or two strands have broken, play it safe and replace the cable.

When squeezing the levers and twisting the throttle on and off, do you notice any binding of the cables as they slide within their housings? Maybe the cables just need lubed. But they may have sharp bends throughout their length that restrict free movement.

Carefully follow the cable housing to see that they've no sharp kinks anywhere. Reroute them, if necessary. Oftentimes the throttle cable will become trapped between the steering head and the fork stop. In time, the housing and the cable will wear through. So beware!

A disc-brake bike will usually have its master cylinder mounted on the handlebar. Unless there's a leak somewhere, it will rarely require topping-up. Doesn't hurt to check it from time to time, though.

Do all the light switches function? Checking lights should be included in your preflight inspection before every ride. Bulb filaments blow at the most awkward times. Incidentally, it's a good idea to carry extra bulbs for both the headlight and taillight. You never know. Carry an extra fuse, too. Though this is a small point, make sure the handgrips are on tight. Imagine what could happen should one pop off when you are laying over for a fast turn.

The Engine Area

Here there are several things to go over. You could start off by checking the engine mounts. If they're not tight, they'll cause severe vibration. Depending on when you've done it last, you should get out your wrenches and go over the various nuts and bolts.

Check underneath the gas tank for leaks. Vibration can cause small hairline cracks in the seams of the tank, allowing gas to drip onto the engine.

Does the engine oil need topping-up? Have you been changing it regularly? Same goes for other oil reservoirs like the gearbox and primary chaincase, if your bike is so designed. When you do change oil, don't overlook the fork legs. Changing oil regularly and keeping it topped up is important.

If your bike has a wet clutch, be sure to use only a lightweight oil, or the plates will stick together. Then you get a dragging clutch and noisy gear changes.

Keeping after the battery is another important, but often neglected, aspect of maintenance. When topping-up the cells, use only distilled water. Tap water contains impurities that can bridge between the battery's plates and cause short-circuiting. Add just enough water to cover the tops of the plates; more than that and it'll seep out through the vent holes in the caps and corrode nearby metal parts.

Keep the battery dry and clean near the terminals, or corrosion will form and, in time, short the battery out from the rest of the circuit. Dab a bit of Vaseline or other lubricant onto the terminals to prevent corrosion.

Because vibration can shorten the life of the battery, place rubber pads underneath it, or take a piece of old inner tube and wrap around it.

A motorcycle battery can discharge quickly, if it's left idle for any length of time. A worthwhile investment is a one- or two-amp trickle charger that can be hooked up to the battery whenever it's not in service for any lengthy period. Don't use automotive charging equipment. Their high-amperage rates can cook a motorcycle battery quickly.

Be careful when carrying tools in the vicinity of the battery. It's possible that a wrench or a screwdriver can bridge the terminals and short out the battery.

Although it's beyond the scope of this book to get into the intricacies of tune-ups, you should keep your bike in sharp tune all the time. If it's beyond your skill to set the valves and ignition timing, to adjust the carburetor, and to undertake the countless other adjustments to keep the engine performing right, have the work done by someone skilled.

Your two-wheeler's maneuverability and responsiveness depend on all its parts working together. The last thing you want is a motorcycle that gets spastic when you turn up the wick. More than one bike rider has avoided a potential accident because his machine responded instantly to a twist of the throttle.

Before we move over to the rear-wheel assembly, make sure the footrest mountings are tight. The last thing you need is a loose footrest giving way under your weight.

The Rear Wheel

Well, here we are, getting near the end of our little tour of the two-wheeler.

Back here components receive their share of abuse and neglect. The rear tire is subject to more wear than the front tire simply because it has the job of delivering engine power to the ground. In the process, it has a lot of its tread scrubbed off. Then add braking and cornering forces to that, and you can readily see what the rear tire has to contend with.

To keep the rear tire from wearing irregularly and "tracking" off to the side, the rear wheel must be centered in the swing-arm fork.

Unless some part of the frame has been bent, most rear-wheel "misalignment" results from careless chain-tension adjustment. Each wheel adjuster must be turned an equal number of turns to keep the wheel centered.

There are several ways to check rear-wheel alignment. The simplest and perhaps most effective is to carefully measure the distance between the axle and the swing-arm pivot (on both sides, of course). This method is effective as long as the rest of the frame and front-fork assembly are perfectly true.

Other ways we'll look at necessitate the front wheel point dead ahead, with the bike sitting level.

Since most motorcycles have wider rear tires than front tires, compensation must be allowed for the extra width of the rear tire.

You might try laying a straight board alongside the tires. Allowance for the different-width tires can be made as follows: first, the board should be high enough off the ground so it can rest against the lower sides of the tires. If the rear tire is one-half inch wider than the front tire, you can either tack a one-fourth-inch strip of wood onto the section of the board that rests against the front tire, or you can cut a one-fourth-inch strip away from the board where it touches the rear tire. If you don't modify the board, you'll need to carefully measure the gaps between the sides of the front tire and the board.

You might try a piece of string. By tying it to a spoke on the rear wheel and pulling it taut from the front of the bike, you can sight along it. But it must be resting against the sides of the rear tire, taking care not to "bend" it. Then carefully check the gaps between the string and the sides of the front tire. If the string is closer to one side of the tire than the other side, you'll have to use a rear-wheel adjuster to center the rear wheel.

If you've a good eye, you can sight along both wheels from either the rear or the front of the machine. But this method takes practice.

Rear-tire balance isn't as critical as the front tire, but it still pays to balance both. To do so means you'll have to disconnect the rear chain.

While you're involved with the rear tire, grasp the wheel at diametrical points and try to shake it to see if there's any wear in the wheel bearings or swing-arm-pivot bushings. Any play here means your bike isn't going to handle well.

To many motorcyclists, the conventional chain-and-sprocket setup used on two-wheelers is one of the more distasteful parts of maintenance. Chains are dirty and noisy and need more care than a shaft-drive system.

Yet the chain-and-sprocket setup is remarkably efficient. And

Worn wheel bearings and rear-swing-arm bushings can be detected by shaking rear wheel with both hands.

its compact design makes it ideal for motorcycles. It's an advantage for the performance buff who likes to change gearing ratios by trying different-size sprockets.

A chain requires two forms of maintenance: adequate lubrication and proper tensioning. Neglect either, and you'll end up replacing the chain long before you should!

Frequent lubrication with a special chain lubricant will keep the chain from drying out and wearing prematurely. It'll also help to force dirt out from the chain's innards where it can do the most harm. Every so often, remove the chain and wash it in a solventlike kerosene.

The second part of chain maintenance is to keep it tensioned properly. As a rule, with rider weight on the seat, there should be three-fourth-inch vertical slack midway between the sprockets at the chain's tightest point of rotation. To find that tightest point, you'll have to rotate the rear wheel. The more

(Above) Chain tension is important, too. There should be about ¾-inch slack, midway between the sprockets with rider weight on the seat, about 1¾-inch with no rider weight. (Below) During your safety inspection, check to see that the spring clip on the master link is well seated and that it's closed and "leads" in the direction of chain travel. Note: Some motorcycles have "endless" rear chains, which have no master link.

worn the chain, the more a chain will vary between tightness and slackness.

A quick indication of chain wear is to grasp the chain at axle height and lift it off the sprocket. If more than two-thirds the height of the teeth can be cleared, the chain has outlived its usefulness.

Don't forget to check the sprockets for worn teeth. If they are pointed, hooked, or, worse, worn to nubs, replace them. Chances are that if the rear-wheel sprocket is worn, so is the gearbox sprocket. Why? The gearbox sprocket, or countershaft sprocket, is the driving member and under more stress; therefore, it wears faster. It's a good idea to replace both sprockets and the chain together. Never put a chain on worn sprockets, and vice versa.

Space doesn't permit a rundown of every step to keep your bike safe. Rather, the intention has been to spur you on to getting into the habit of going over your bike frequently. Get to know what makes your bike tick. The more you know about it, the more you'll appreciate it.

7

Motorcycle Mastery

If you find your throttle hand developing a twitch, don't get alarmed; it's just reacting to your eager anticipation of what's to come.

Back to Basics

Before you entertain visions of concrete ribbons beckoning you on, let's go back to basics. If you're a beginner, you'll have the advantage of learning good habits right from the beginning. If you're an experienced rider, you probably know what we're about to cover. So, if you find yourself yawning, you might want to go on to the next chapter. Then again, maybe your curiosity is piqued just enough to make you want to continue. In any event, let's start off with mounting a motorcycle. Most cyclists mount from the left side, because it's the most natural, for some reason. And most bikes have their kickstands mounted on that side, so the bikes lean toward the left.

When you swing your right leg over the seat, *make sure you apply the front brake.* Why? By not applying the front brake, there's always a chance you'll lose your balance if the bike starts moving forward suddenly. And it's pretty embarrassing to find yourself flat on your face from a zero-speed spill.

When you've mounted up and are sitting there fastening your helmet or whatever, *keep your foot on the rear brake pedal.* Doing so will keep the bike from shifting around and, again, possibly spilling.

When you dismount, apply the front brake.

Okay, before you climb back on and kick that steel-and-rubber hunk into life, here's a couple of tips on maneuvering without it running. A lightweight cycle is easy to maneuver. You can stand alongside it and push or pull it without any trouble, or you can straddle it and paddle around.

But moving a 350-pound bike is a little trickier, especially if you're small. The secret here is to stand alongside the bike, to hold onto the grips, and to brace yourself against it.

If you're sitting on it and want to back it up against a slight grade, apply the front brake and thrust yourself forward. Then immediately snap your body weight backward, at the same time releasing the brake.

How to "Fire" It Up

One of the appealing features of modern motorcycles is the electric starter. It has civilized motorcycles for many persons who dislike having to kickstart a big-capacity bike into life. But kickstarting a motorcycle is not the bugaboo a lot of people make it out to be.

If the proper technique is used and the bike is in reasonably good tune, it shouldn't take more than three or four kicks to "light off" even a cold engine. A warm engine should take even fewer kicks. A high-performance, radically tuned engine is something else. But what we're concerned with here is most stock-type bikes.

If you've ridden different bikes, you know that each has its own starting quirks. Take two exact machines: one may require the throttle to be slightly open to start; the other may require its throttle closed. Some carburetors must be flooded; others must not. After you've become familiar with a bike, you'll learn the proper way to start it.

To start a motorcycle easily, you must first have it supported properly. There are several ways to support a bike to keep it from falling over on you. Let's look at them.

A lightweight bike can be easily started by standing alongside it and "fanning" the kickstarter with just the leg. Bigger bikes are something else. Depending on your size and the capacity of the engine, you'll probably want to support the bike on either its centerstand or its kickstand.

The kickstand doesn't offer as firm a base as does the centerstand. And it can be awkward to start the bike if the kickstand is resting on a cambered surface. You can lose your balance, too. Besides, repeated usage of the kickstand will cause it to break off on some models. Providing the motorcycle is resting on a level surface, the centerstand will give the best support.

Once you become familiar with starting your bike, you might learn to start it by just supporting it with your leg opposite the kickstarter side, as you straddle the seat. Lean the bike slightly toward the support leg to maintain your balance. Then move the kickstarter about one-third to one-half of its total travel. You'll probably find it easier to do this after first pulling in the clutch lever. Once you've positioned the kickstarter down as mentioned, release the clutch lever. Now raise up on your support leg and then bring your full weight down on the kickstarter, straightening the kicking leg as you bring it down. As the kickstarter approaches the lower end of its travel, try to increase the speed and thrust force of your leg.

Learning how to start your bike without resorting to the centerstand or kickstand is a technique that can stand you in good stead should you ever stall your bike in traffic. You save valuable time by not having to fuss with putting your bike on its stand, thereby minimizing the possibility of some impetuous driver running over you.

If you can't start your bike with the kickstarter, try coasting down a hill or pushing it briskly and then hopping aboard. Make sure it's in third gear or more; if you let the clutch out with the transmission in low gear, the engine will act as a brake. Then you must start all over.

Although most larger motorcycles today are multi-cylinder types, there are some single-cylinder or "big lunger" types available.

If you ever try to kickstart a big-capacity, four-stroke single the way you do a small, lightweight twin, you better have either the leg of an elephant or a couple of cement blocks strapped to your back. Kicking a big single over in a half-hearted manner will make you feel as though you've been on a pogo-stick. Worse yet, it may kick back, giving you the impression that your bike has a built-in ejection seat.

To kickstart a big single easily, the trick is to get the piston in the right direction. That is, the piston should be raised past the compression stroke to where it's just starting back down. If you try to kickstart while the piston is rising on the compression stroke, the compressed intake charge resists the upward movement of the piston. Most large-capacity singles have a device known as a compression release to facilitate starting. On a four-stroker this compression release opens the exhaust valve so the piston can be easily moved past the compression stroke with the aid of the kickstarter.

If the compression release is used properly, starting a big single is no more difficult than starting a multi-cylinder bike. Before operating the compression release, pump the kickstarter until resistance is felt. That indicates the piston is up against compression. Now pull in the compression-release lever and carefully move the kickstarter down a few inches. Release the lever. Then follow through with a full, rapid swing of the kickstarter to spin the engine over. If the engine is in tune, it should fire up.

Another way to get the piston past compression without a

compression release is to pump the kickstarter as before to bring the piston up to compression. Then repeatedly stroke the kickstarter just hard enough to bring the piston past top dead center. As before, follow through with a rapid kick.

If these two techniques don't work, "bump start" the engine by coasting down a hill or by running with the bike as fast as you can, hopping on, and putting it into gear. Once you've started the engine, warm it up before taking off. Taking off with a cold engine is not only dangerous (it may stall under load), but it creates unnecessary wear because the oil hasn't had a chance to circulate thoroughly.

If the engine hasn't been shut off very long before you restart it, allow at least thirty seconds or so to give the oil a chance to circulate. As soon as an engine is shut off, oil starts draining off the cylinder walls and other load-bearing surfaces.

Getting to Know Your Bike

Now you're ready to start "feeling out" your bike by experimenting with various control techniques.

Interestingly, the little techniques you pick up have a cumulative effect on your riding style. Learn the right techniques, and you master your motorcycle; learn the wrong techniques, and the motorcycle masters you.

One of the earmarks of an expert cyclist is that he operates his bike so fluidly that he and his bike seem like some mechanical centaur. They merge together.

Before you start putting your bike through its paces, you want to make sure that you have plenty of room to ride in. Find an empty parking lot or a fairly large field relatively free of rocks, bumps, and holes. Stay away from public roads. You can't concentrate on your riding, if you have to worry about some car or truck running into you.

Right here is a good place to mention a couple things that you should have drilled into your head. Never start off

For getting the feel of your bike, find a deserted parking lot or smooth dirt field and then experiment with different riding positions and control techniques.

without glancing over your shoulder to see what's coming. Even if you're the only one around, look over your shoulder. Later this precaution may make the difference in your pulling safely away from the curb or your lane of traffic and having some vehicle sideswipe you. If you don't make this precaution a habit, you might forget to check for other vehicles someday as you pull out.

You're probably thinking, "This guy's repeating himself. He mentioned that before." That's right! And you'll see it mentioned again later on. It's that important.

Besides glancing over your shoulder, make sure your kickstand is retracted before starting off. Another thing that might seem unnecessary to mention. But unless you've taken off in a hurry and forgot to pull up the kickstand and wound up on the ground from the kickstand catching on something, you might not realize how easy it is to have an accident this way.

Mull over those two precautions for a while. They could save you a lot of skin later.

A lot of your control depends on how you sit on the bike. If you've set up your bike for street riding as described in

Although you may never wish to become this skilled a rider, it does show you the skill that is possible to develop with a motorcycle. But it takes the right mental attitude combined with practice, practice, practice. *(Courtesy Yamaha International Corp.)*

Chapter 5, you'll be seated with the upper body bent slightly forward and the hands resting on the grips. The shoulders will be a bit hunched, with the elbows jutting out somewhat. The feet should be resting on the footrests parallel to the ground. If the toes hang down sharply over the footrests, there's a chance they could catch on the ground during a sharp turn. The knees should snuggle up to the gas tank.

Should you have to brace yourself for a bump, try posting slightly on the footrests and gripping the gas tank with your knees. This helps you keep your balance and stabilizes the bike. If your machine has a narrow gas tank, it may be uncomfortable trying to keep the knees against the tank, however. But try to keep them as close to the tank as possible.

When posting, or bracing yourself against the footrests, your feet won't dislodge so easily if you keep the footrests wedged in between the heels and soles of your footgear.

With the proper seating position, your center of gravity (CG) will be close to the motorcycle's CG, which is near the middle of the bike. The lower the bike's CG, the more stable it is. A high CG means the motorcycle is top heavy. Another

Learning to "wheelie" a bike can be a lot of fun, but it takes considerable practice and skill to do it without having the bike flip back over. Lightweight motorcycles lend themselves well to "popping wheelies." *(Courtesy Kawasaki Motor Corp.)*

factor that effects the bike's CG is the amount of gas in the tank. A full tank will raise the CG, which will effect handling.

Your body's CG, together with the motorcycle's CG, results in a combined CG that can be altered by the way in which you sit on the seat or stand on the footrests. Normally, for street riding, you'll ride while seated. By sliding your weight forward or backward, you can change the horizontal location of the combined CG.

You can alter the vertical location of the combined CG by raising your body off the seat. In effect, when you stand on the footrests, you raise the combined CG because your body's CG is poised at a higher point from the motorcycle's CG. When you're seated, your weight is positioned closer to seat level, making for a lower combination CG.

It's amazing how much you can learn about a motorcycle's handling just by undertaking some simple maneuvers. For instance, when a two-wheeler's speed falls less than ten miles per hour, you must rely on your sense of balance and skill to keep the bike up. The less the speed, the more the bike will wander from side to side in an effort to stabilize. And the more demands it'll make on you.

Under such conditions you have to use Body English, that is, positioning yourself off center to maintain balance of the bike. Although Body English is used more by off-road riders, it still has some value for the street jockey.

After all, in heavy, city traffic, you may have to change direction quickly. By shifting your weight to one side, you can maneuver the machine sharply without losing your sense of balance or control.

With Body English your body becomes a lever that exerts force against the motorcycle.

Body English has more effect on your bike when you're poised on the footrests than when you're seated. When you're up on the footrests, you place your CG farther away from the motorcycle's CG, so your body has more leverage to work with against the machine. If you're making a tight, low-speed turn to the right, move your body to the left to counteract the force of gravity trying to pull the bike over on its right side.

With Body English you can sit or stand on the footrests and lean the bike. Or you can lean off center, while holding the bike vertically.

Try it.

Get moving just fast enough to keep from wandering around. Then bear down on, say, the right footrest, and press your left knee against the gas tank. If you're seated, depending on the size and speed of the motorcycle, it will lean slightly to the right. Complement the pressure on the footrest and gas tank with a downward pressure on the right handgrip. The bike will lean more to the right. If you *pull up* farther on the left handgrip, the bike will bank even more sharply than before. If you stand on the footrests and perform all the above motions together, the bike will veer sharply to the right. Be careful when trying this. Overdo it, and you could spill.

The faster you go, the less effect Body English will have on your bike, due to the resistance from gyroscopic inertia and tire alignment.

At speeds more than thirty miles per hour, pushing down or pulling up on the handgrips will produce enough leverage against the bike to make it veer to one side. This veering action can help you on the road when you suddenly come upon an obstacle.

Let's say that you suddenly come upon a large rock. You snap the handlebar to the side with a push/pull action on the grips, and the bike leans away from you. As you zip by the rock, you instantly push/pull on the grips again in the other direction to keep the bike on course. It's a good idea to practice this technique before you try it out on the road.

Another way to practice Body English is to undertake a series of tight turns by moving your bike spirally. At first, start out by making a fairly wide turn. Each successive time around

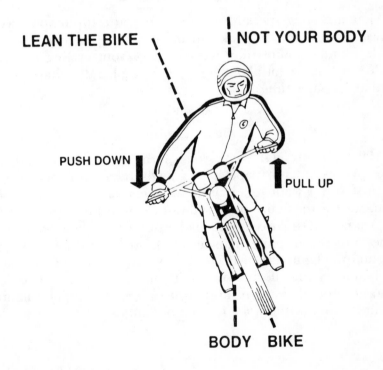

Quick turn technique.

gradually tighten up the turn radius. As the spiral becomes tighter, your speed decreases and you find yourself leaning more toward the outside of the turn to balance your bike. See how tightly you can turn without putting your foot down or stalling out.

With practice, you'll be able to make full-lock turns, as you "hang out" to the side to keep your bike from falling in toward the center of the turn.

When riding the bike, keep your feet up on the footrests. Dragging your feet not only looks sloppy, but reduces control of the bike. As soon as you get underway without wobbling, get those feet up.

Some Special Exercises

Here are some special exercises that you can put your two-wheeler through. To make them more challenging, have a little friendly competition with some of your cycling friends. You can learn a lot about how your bike handles and have a ball at the same time.

Figure Eight

Make a figure eight with some form of boundary markers like pylons or even paper plates held down with something. At first you'll want to space the markers far enough apart so you can cut the figure eight without too much difficulty. Then as your skill increases, gradually tighten up the boundary lines until you must maneuver almost at full-lock to get around the figure eight. If you knock over or ride on a marker or boundary line, deduct points, if you're competing. If you're not, go around it again, until you can cut the tightest figure eight possible without getting out of bounds.

Slalom

Here you set up a line of cones, pylons, or whatever

The slalom exercise is ideal for learning how to use Body English to control your bike under awkward conditions. As you gain skill, gradually reduce distance between pylons.

between two boundary lines, no closer to each other than the turning radius of your bike. The distance between the cones can be varied according to the skill of the rider(s) and the size of the bike(s). The idea is to weave in and out of the cones, turn around at the other end, and go back through. If you can go through the slalom without crossing the boundary lines, tighten up the distance between the cones.

The slalom is excellent for learning how to use Body English in tight turning. It's a variation of the figure eight.

Line Stop

To perform this exercise, you'll need a series of parallel

lines, placed a few feet apart. The boundary lines of parking-lot stalls are ideal.

The idea is to start at one end of the "line of lines" and go to the other end by stopping the bike so the front tire rests on each line momentarily, maintaining balance without putting a foot down, and then taking off again to stop the front tire on the next line.

To make it more difficult, place boundary lines on either side, a couple of feet apart. Later, to make it even more difficult, place each line several yards apart, space permitting, and increase your speed.

This exercise teaches precision braking and balance.

Slow Race

The object in this exercise is to go as slow as possible without losing your balance or stalling the engine. With boundary lines on each side, ride fifty to seventy-five feet. It's especially fun when you compete. The *last* one to the finish line without losing his balance is the winner. You also must stay within the boundary lines.

This exercise tests your balance and coordination of throttle and clutch.

Plank Ride

Lay a six-to-eight-inch plank of any length on the ground, and try to ride your bike on it. As skill increases, narrow the width of the plank down to four to five inches. For a real skill test, you can make a teeter-totter by placing a brick or two under the middle of the plank.

As an alternative to the plank, try drawing a line with chalk on an asphalt parking lot. Two sections of rope can also be used for boundaries, the idea being to ride within the boundaries. To make it even more difficult, lay out the ropes in an S pattern. It takes skill to stay within the ropes.

Another exercise for developing control is to see how far you can ride on a two-by-four or straight line without wandering off course.

There are many variations of the exercises covered. Use your imagination to come up with more. Their primary purpose is to provide you means for developing your riding skills by "feeling out" your bike under different conditions. Such exercises aren't only constructive; they're fun, too. After all, that's one of the reasons we ride motorcycles.

8

The ABCs of Braking and Cornering

Lack of skill in either braking or cornering considerably increases your chances for becoming an unwanted fender ornament or an unnatural inhabitant of a tree. If you could analyze the accidents that befall motorcyclists, you'd find that many happen to bikers who don't know how to stop quickly and safely, or who run off the road during cornering. Such motorcyclists are victims of their own wrongdoing. So, if you want to be a well-rounded riding expert, learn your ABCs of braking and cornering.

Braking

Braking a motorcycle requires a lot more finesse than it does with a dual-track vehicle. After all, you don't have the margin for error regarding traction loss that the motorist has. Slap the binders on too hard, and your tires don't have to skid very far to put you down.

Once you learn how to haul your bike down from speed in the shortest possible distance, you'll have the advantage of outstopping other vehicles. The motorcycle's independent braking systems provide a high degree of stopping power that other vehicles don't have. With disc-type brakes becoming more popular, braking efficiency is even better. Disc brakes aren't as susceptible to fading from repeated usage and water as are drum brakes.

Regardless of the type of brake used, the trick to braking is to apply optimum pressure without locking up the brake(s) and skidding.

Whether a brake locks up or not depends a lot on the surface conditions. Braking imprudently on a slippery surface or unstable surface (stones, sand, leaves, etc.) is a good way to end up embracing *terra firma*.

If there's one basic rule for braking a motorcycle, it's *do it when the bike is upright*.

There's no quicker way to part company with Ol' Paint than to jam the brakes on when you're heeled over for a turn. And that's where the sloppy rider hits trouble. He'll speed into a turn only to realize at the last instant that he's going too fast. Out of panic, he slaps the brakes on, only to find himself sliding across the road. The expert, on the other hand, will decelerate his bike *before* he enters the turn.

Now, it's possible to feather the brakes lightly while moderately banked, but it takes a sensitive touch to keep the tires from breaking traction. Play it safe and brake before entering the turn.

To the novice rider, it may seem hard to believe that seventy-five percent of the motorcycle's stopping power is provided by the front brake. But it's true. It works this way: the braking force applied to the front tire's contact point is counteracted by an inertial reaction about the combined (bike/rider) CG. The braking force at the contact point is acting rearward, while the combined weight of the bike and its operator is pivoting about the combined CG to make the front end of the motorcycle "sink." This phenomenon of braking is called weight transference. When the rear brake is applied by itself, weight transference still takes place, but to a lesser degree. The rear tire's contact point is behind the combination CG, so it induces less of a reaction.

Despite the front brake's greater power of the two brakes, many riders never use it advantageously. For one thing, they fear locking up the front wheel and flipping over the handlebar. Expert riders know differently. Even with today's powerful brakes, it's near impossible to "take a trip" over the handlebar from an overly hard application of the front brake. Of course, there's always the danger of using the front brake indiscreetly on an unstable surface.

Anyway, just what is the best way to bring a bike to a quick stop? Expert riders feel that using both brakes together with gearing down is the quickest, most stable way. By gearing down as you apply the brakes, you are taking advantage of a "third" brake—engine compression. The lower the gear you downshift into, the greater becomes the retarding effect of engine compression. Four-stroke engines have greater compression than two-stroke engines, however.

By applying the rear brake slightly before the front one, stopping stability may be improved somewhat.

To become proficient at braking takes practice. There's a fine line between maximum-effective pressure on the brakes and brake lock-up. What happens when you lock up the brakes? If the front brake locks up, the front wheel becomes unsteerable and the tire slides away from its intended path. Should the rear brake lock up at high speed, the tire breaks traction and the whole rear-wheel assembly "speeds up" relative to the bike's forward speed.

Because the motorcycle is hinged at the steering head, the accelerating rear-wheel unit can cause the bike to jackknife.

If the rear brake locks up, you have a better chance to recover stability. Regardless which brake it is, if it locks, release it immediately. Always remember that a sliding tire is unstable in all directions. The only way it can regain its stability is for the wheel to start turning again.

To familiarize yourself with braking your bike, go back to that empty parking lot or field you used in the last chapter, remember?

Start with fairly low speeds, around fifteen to twenty miles per hour. Experiment by using each brake by itself and with each other. Try braking without gearing down and then with it. Notice the difference in stopping distance when both brakes are used together with engine compression.

As your skill increases in decelerating your bike in the shortest-possible distance, gradually increase the speed. Don't go up to higher speeds until you've mastered braking at the lower speeds. You will become progressively accustomed to your bike's braking and handling nature. If the brakes start getting "spongy" from overheating, let them cool.

The harder drum brakes are worked, the less effective they'll be. The drums expand, preventing the linings from making full contact.

Needless to say, whenever you ride a strange bike, become thoroughly familiar with its brakes.

Cornering

In cornering, the motorcycle becomes multi-dimensional in its movement, much like that of an airplane in flight. However, as mentioned earlier, the motorcycle's closeness to the ground provides more awareness of motion.

However stimulating it may be, cornering makes certain demands on a motorcyclist. You must judge the speed at which the turn can be made. If you go into the turn too fast, centrifugal force will pull you off the road. If you don't have enough speed, and you bank abruptly, gravity will overpower centrifugal force. Furthermore, you must know the surface conditions to determine the best line to follow around the curve.

Normally when you go into a turn, you lean your body to move the bike off center. If it's a tight turn, you may use Body English to bank the bike.

The motorcycle can also be made to corner by sitting in a normal seating position and by pushing on one end of the handlebar grip, *parallel to the ground.* Let's say you want to turn left. As you get to the point where you're ready to lay the bike over, you push on the left grip, so that the handlebar is angled to the direction of forward travel and the front wheel is pointing toward the right side. But the rest of the motorcycle is still pointing and traveling straight ahead. Centrifugal force then pulls the bike over to the left, making it lean. Almost immediately gyroscopic precession and the tire alignment forces get into the act, too, by snapping the front wheel back

The professional racing motorcyclist must be an expert at cornering, if he's to win his share of races. Although you won't necessarily "lay" a bike over the way he does, you must still become skilled enough to corner without losing control and spilling. *(Courtesy Yamaha International Corp.)*

toward center and over to the left side. The next thing you know, your bike is cornering to the left.

On a well-designed motorcycle, cornering is almost an automatic action. It's as though the bike has a built-in brain, programmed to take a turn. That's partly true, because if a motorcycle has the right steering geometry, it will uncannily select the right combination of lean angle and turn radius to match its speed. If, however, the bike has poor handling, its rider must wrestle it around the turn.

A lot of factors contribute to the way a two-wheeler takes a turn. The gyroscopic properties of the wheels have the principal role of keeping the bike upright, of course. Plus the geometry of the fork assembly and frame together with the distortional properties of the tires enter into the matter. Also, the location of the bike's CG and of the rider's CG have a lot to do with the way the motorcycle behaves when it's laid over. As a rule, the lower the CG(s), the more stable the bike will be in a turn. The tread design and the composition of the tread are other factors that help to determine a motorcycle's cornering capabilities.

Hard cornering can bring out flaws in a bike's handling that otherwise wouldn't be noticeable under straight-ahead running. A motorcycle may be rock-steady when traveling dead ahead. Yet, when it's laid over for a turn, it may suddenly become very "twitchy" and unstable.

Cornering wobble is the term usually applied to a motorcycle that acts as though it's made of rubber on a turn. Cornering places severe stress on the frame and suspension. For the conservative rider, there's no problem around turns. But for the hotshoe who barrels into a turn kamikaze style, flaws in the bike's design and construction soon show up.

Such a bike may "shake its head" just enough to warn its operator that he'd better take it easy. Then again, it may be ornery enough to "spit him off" before he has a chance to bring it under control. That's the reason you should take time to learn your bike's cornering behavior.

Like braking, learning to corner well requires practice. Again, go back to your empty parking lot or smooth field, and practice cornering at different speeds. Learn how far you can lay your mount over before it kisses the ground. Knowing exactly how far you can lean your two-wheeler is critical to mastering cornering. The indifferent rider may never learn his bike's point of no return, until it rewards him with a none-too-gentle spill.

When you're practicing cornering, cut low-speed turns at first. It may even help to use Body English for those slow, tight-radius turns. The sharper the turn, the more you need to lean your weight to the outside of the turn. But as you increase the speed for successive turns, lean with the bike, gingerly feeling your machine's point of *almost* no return.

To master cornering, you must recognize two pitfalls that accompany fast cornering: you can either run off the outside of the curve, or you can lean too far in and drop the bike. Let's look at these two hazardous consequences in more detail.

For a motorcycle to undertake a stable turn, two forces must balance each other: gravity and centrifugal force. If you enter a turn too slowly or bank too far, gravity will overpower centrifugal force. If you take a turn too fast, centrifugal force will overcome gravity. In most cases, you'll corner at high-enough speeds to preclude the possibility of your bike falling over.

If the curve is shallow and your speed isn't too great, you may be able to upright the bike just long enough to apply the brakes and scrub off some speed. If you're smart, you'll scrub off that speed before you get to the curve, when the bike is still in an upright position.

As you approach a curve and start slowing down, get into the lowest gear possible that will allow you to keep some power as you take the curve. By keeping on some power, the motorcycle stays stable. If you rush up to a curve, jam on the brakes, and then alternately apply the brakes and throttle as you take the curve, you'll upset the motorcycle's innate stability.

Instead of following a smooth path around the curve, it'll jerk all over the road and possibly skitter out from under you.

Besides taking a curve at the right speed, you must always maintain the right position on the road. If you approach the curve properly, follow the right path around it, and exit the curve the right way, you'll find that even sharp turns aren't a hassle. By maintaining the right position throughout the turn, you'll minimize centrifugal force at higher cornering speeds.

Because excessive speed is the reason a lot of cyclists get into trouble when cornering, let's see how to cope with it.

A motorcycle is a deceptively fast vehicle. If you don't keep an eye on the speedometer, you can soon find yourself going a lot faster than you realize. Then if you suddenly come upon a sharp curve in the road, your speed may be too great for your reflexes and judgment to cope with. Under such conditions you may overshoot the turn or hit the brakes or bank too far, so that the tires break traction. Centrifugal force makes the bike understeer or travel more in a tangent or straight line. One way to reduce the pull of centrifugal force is to slow down. But when you enter a sharp curve too fast, you don't have the time to slow down. If you apply the brakes while you're banked over, you know what'll happen.

Besides countering centrifugal force, assuming the right position in cornering has another advantage: it enables you to have a better view around a blind curve. You then have a better chance to take evasive action if slippery spots, oncoming vehicles, or other obstacles suddenly confront you. The more quickly you spot a dangerous situation, the more time you have to avoid it.

For a right-hand turn, approach the curve by moving over to the extreme left *of your side of the road.* If there's no oncoming traffic, however, you can move over to the left farther. As you reach approximately the halfway point of the turn, gradually drift over toward the right, so that as you exit the turn, you're near the right side of the road.

If it's a left-hand turn, approach by staying well toward the right-hand side of the road. As you near the halfway point, gradually move over toward the center of the road. Don't drift into the other lane.

By cutting the flattest arc possible through the turn, you minimize centrifugal force, while permitting yourself a better view of the road ahead.

Of course, surface conditions, traffic, and obstacles will dictate your exact path. So study the curve ahead as far as you can. You may have to deviate from your intended path somewhat to avoid trouble.

The key to safe cornering is to first get your speed down before you enter the turn, using the brakes together with downshifting of the gears. With a four-stroke-engined motorcycle, you can often slow enough by just downshifting. A two-stroke engine is different. It doesn't provide enough compression to slow the bike down. So the brakes must be used harder. If you've been riding four-strokers and then go to a two-stroke machine, get familiar with its deceleration capabilities before you do any serious cornering.

More than one two-stroke rider has run off a curve simply because he mistakenly depended on engine compression to slow him down.

Heaven forbid, what will you do if you ever take a turn too fast and find the bike sliding out? If it's the front tire skidding, it will probably drop you without a warning. If it's the rear tire, you have a chance to regain control.

If the rear tire were to slide out first, instinctively you'd snap the throttle shut. This would be about the same as hitting the brake, because it would transmit a sudden jolt to the already delicate bond between the tire and the road. And the tire would probably slide away even faster.

Your best bet, if you react quickly enough, is to "hotshoe" your bike around the turn, that is, put your turn-side foot on the ground for support and ease the gas on. The handlebar will have to be turned in the direction the rear end is sliding, until control can be regained. Such a technique is often referred to by professional racers as being "crossed up." But if you use your head and keep your speed within reason when cornering, you won't ever have to make sure of such a hairy technique to control a skid.

Other than the extreme example just mentioned, keep your feet on the footrests during cornering. As mentioned earlier, dragging a foot around a turn shows lack of confidence and poor riding technique. What's more, it interferes with the balance and control of the motorcycle.

When you master braking and cornering, you're well on your way to becoming an expert. But don't be deluded into thinking that you can take shortcuts. It takes lots of practice to haul that two-wheeler down from high speeds just short of locking up the brakes, or to lay it over for a high-speed turn without spilling.

Beware of overconfidence. It's a one-way trip to trouble.

9
On the Road

Linked to braking and cornering is the subject of road conditions.

How well you stop or bank (or run upright, for that matter) depends significantly on surface conditions. Because of the motorcycle's single-track nature, you have no choice but to become an expert at "reading the road." Whether it's determining the traction of a particular surface or the way in which a road is laid out, you must learn how to "read" a variety of road conditions.

Reading the Road

As with learning how to operate a motorcycle, learning how to read surface conditions requires awareness. Despite today's high-traction tires and improved suspension systems, you can still skid on unstable surfaces.

So, constantly read road conditions and adjust your speed

and riding style accordingly. Cultivate awareness of and sensitivity to the road.

Aside from paying more attention to surface conditions from behind the handlebar, eyeball them firsthand. Park and feel the road with your hand. Notice the texture of the surface. Is there any substance on it that would effect traction? Can your tires ride on such a surface? If it's dry, imagine what it would be like if it were wet. In other words, try to relate to that surface from the standpoint of a tire's contact point.

By taking time to study the surface, you'll notice far more of its characteristics than you would from just riding.

Obviously, you're not going to screech to a halt and jump off your bike to run your hand over the surface every time you come across a different road. But by studying the different kinds of *basic* surfaces firsthand, you'll learn about surface conditions. And you'll be able to readily identify those surface conditions from behind the handlebar.

The more you study surface conditions, the more efficiently your brain's visual/thinking centers will pick up details that normally you'd never notice.

Most modern roads are constructed either of asphalt or concrete. As can be imagined, there are many variations of them regarding their surface textures. Unless it's worn smooth, asphalt will generally have a more coarse texture than concrete. This coarseness will aid traction, especially when it's raining, because water can drain away, rather than get "trapped."

In winter, during daylight, asphalt won't freeze quite as fast as concrete, because its darker surface absorbs and retains heat better. When the sun disappears, however, asphalt radiates heat quickly. Depending on the road's temperature and the amount of moisture present, freezing conditions can occur rapidly.

Older, well-traveled asphalt roads often become "polished" or smoothly textured, thereby offering less traction. Then there's tire-wear particles from other vehicles—oil drippings, dirt, sand, leaves, and water. Is it any wonder that a motorcycle can skid?

On older asphalt roads, be on the lookout for tarred sections where repairs have been made. In hot weather, those tarred areas become soft and bubbly. Besides being slippery, they're extremely unstable. Under the weight of a motorcycle, notably during braking and cornering, they'll give way.

Don't overlook the dangers of a newly laid asphalt surface. Until exposure to the elements has had a chance to "weatherbeat" the asphalt, there'll be a certain amount of oiliness to it, coupled with the substances mentioned above, that will induce very slippery conditions.

Concrete will usually have a smoother surface than asphalt. If there's little or no camber to the road, water will stay on the surface, accentuating the concrete's smoothness.

When the temperature is near freezing and there is enough moisture, use caution when traveling on the ramps leading to bridges and on the bridges themselves. These surfaces will freeze more quickly than surrounding roads, because of the cold air circulating around them.

Another type of surface that can make your spine tingle is the steel gratings on bridge floors. A motorcycle has a tendency to weave from side to side when traveling on them. Rather than fight the bike's errant behavior, let it wander a little. Its innate stability knows what to do. The worst thing you can do is to fight the bike. Just keep your speed within reason—not too fast, not too slow. Don't shift your weight around. And go easy on the clutch, gas, and brakes.

If you travel too slowly, the bike may weave even more violently. The slower the wheels are turning, the weaker their gyro effect. So, the more disturbing influence the gratings have on them.

You'll find this the case where there's relatively large spaces between the gratings. Oftentimes just increasing the forward speed smoothly will diminish the weaving action, as the wheels' gyro effect becomes stronger.

If you don't overcontrol, try following a shallow, diagonal path from side to side as you cross the bridge. In other words, let the bike travel in one direction for a while, then gently nudge it back toward the other side. This technique differs from the bike's normal weaving action in that it's of a longer duration, plus you're helping to execute it. This technique can be unnerving to other drivers, so it shouldn't be done with other traffic nearby.

One of the classic hazards is the railroad crossing. Since the first motorcycle sputtered down the road, railroad crossings have been waiting to send unwary riders sliding. The expert cyclist knows that the rails must be approached head-on, so that the motorcycle is as near perpendicular to the rails as it can be.

Often the rails will jut above the road surface so that if the front tire should strike one at an angle, it will slide along the rail instead of crossing it.

Be especially careful of depressions, stones, loose road surfaces, oil deposits, etc., directly in front of the rails. Oil deposits from other vehicles that have waited for passing trains pose another threat. Crossings on secondary roads may have been repaired with stones or tarred sections that can create unstable surface conditions.

When approaching a railroad crossing, slow down enough to where you can read surface conditions and pick the best path over the rails. If they are angled sharply to the road, get your speed well down to where you can line up your bike head-on with them without danger of losing control or swerving to the other side of the road.

Keep the bike upright. Don't shift gears, hit the brakes, or jerk the throttle on or off. Make all your actions smoothly.

No matter where you ride, you'll find an infinite variety of surface conditions that demand your attention and judgment. Out on the freeway, you may run onto a section of road with grooves cut into the surface. Their purpose is to improve traction when it's raining. Although they're effective for channeling water away, they create a steering problem for motorcycles. Those grooves will make a bike wander in much the same manner as the gratings on bridge floors "tug" at the wheels.

Freeway entrance and exit ramps have their own kinds of traction problems. Stay away from the lower banked areas of the ramps, as they're catchalls for all sorts of traction-robbing debris. The entrance ramps will usually have more oil drippings. For that reason never ride in the center areas of the entrance ramps; stay near the higher outside areas. And when traveling up hilly roads, stay to one side of the center of the lane. Trucks and other vehicles labor to get up a hill and deposit heavy concentrations of oil. Oil deposits can also be found at stop signs and red lights.

Additional slippery surfaces are manhole covers, drain gratings, crosswalk markings, and steel expansion joints in bridge floors and ramps.

Secondary roads can be more hazardous than main highways, because they'll often have a greater variety of slippery, unstable surface conditions. Patched sections, potholes, stones, mud, leaves, sand, hay and animal droppings near farms, damp spots caused by overhanging trees, and even dead animals—all pose traction hindrances.

Back roads will usually have more varied surface conditions for a given area than will main roads. Sometimes a secondary paved road will suddenly change into a gravel or dirt road. If you're going fast, you may not have enough time to apply the brakes while still on the pavement. If so, don't hit the brakes and snap the throttle shut when you leave the pavement. Instead, ease back on the gas, and post slightly. The bike will wander around some, but it'll be picking out the best "footing" to remain upright.

If you should suddenly come upon a large rock or a tree limb, and you can't avoid it, hit it straight on. Post slightly, and yank up on the handlebar grips at the same time you gas it. In effect, what you're doing is lightening the front end so that it can climb over the obstacle more readily. If you hit the side of an obstacle with your front wheel, it'll deflect the wheel to the side and throw the bike. After an encounter with a rock or pothole, the bike may get wobbly. Let it stabilize itself; don't hit the brakes. Keep your feet bearing down against the footrests and hold the handlebar firmly, but not lock-armed. Slowly applying throttle will bring the bike out of its "head-shaking." It helps to keep your knees pressed against the gas tank, to help stabilize the bike.

Wet-Road Riding

If you scurry for shelter at the first drop of rain, read on. Although traction is critical on a wet surface, you can travel it safely, *if you use your head.* If you read surface conditions carefully, adjust your speed accordingly, and operate your bike smoothly, wet surfaces shouldn't be the hazard a lot of riders think they are. Your tires also have an important role in wet-road riding.

Anyway, if you want to gain skill and confidence on wet surfaces, do it *progressively.* Sound familiar, that word? And the best way to develop a feel for wet roads is to go back to that paved parking lot or back road. Remember?

With no other traffic around to hassle you, you're ready to get your feet "wet" (figuratively speaking). If you're an experienced rider who has just gotten a new bike, you can get used to it on wet roads easier when you go off by yourself. The last thing you need is some joker in a car who is tailgating you or trying to run you off the road.

A wet road is at its slipperiest when it just starts raining after a dry spell, because the first pattering of rain mixes with all sorts of stuff, like oil drippings, dirt, and tire-wear particles (like microscopic rubber ball bearings) to form a slime film that is the next thing to ice.

Until that film has had a chance to wash away, be extremely careful. If the rain is heavy, it won't take long for the slime to clear off the road. But if it's only drizzle, tiptoe over the road. Stay out of the center of well-traveled traffic lanes.

There's another phenomenon called hydroplaning that can get you into trouble, too. When you skid, the tires are still in contact with the road. But when you hydroplane, the tires separate, either partially or totally, from the road surface because a layer of water causes the tires to actually skim, or plane, over the road.

Hydroplaning is directly related to the motorcycle's speed and to the depth of water on the road. Other factors involved are the tread's design and depth and the width of the tires. If a motorcycle is traveling fast enough, there doesn't have to be a great deal of water present. And with today's high-powered motorcycles running on high-traction tires, it's easy to go faster than what common sense dictates.

A rule-of-thumb means for determining if there's enough water on the road to cause hydroplaning is to observe the raindrops hitting the surface. If they make a splashing or "dimpling" effect on the surface water, then hydroplaning is possible.

If the road surface is coarse and cambered, so that water is channeled away, there's less chance for skidding or hydroplaning. You can further reduce the threat of hydroplaning by riding in the tire tracks or "wipe" areas of the vehicle in front of you, as its tires squeegee water away.

More traction is provided by an asphalt surface where imbedded stones protrude above surface water. What makes a wet road so treacherous are oil and gasoline deposits. Gas is slipperier than water and next to invisible on a wet surface. Be extra careful when you're riding by gas stations or garages.

In the fall, you'll encounter still another potentially dangerous situation—leaves. They can be bad enough when dry; but when wet, they're extremely slippery.

And, for pete's sake, stay clear of manhole covers and drain gratings. Although you can't avoid them, take it easy on steel expansion strips on bridges and on crosswalk markers. Keep the throttle, clutch, and front-brake cables well oiled and free of kinks, so that they move freely. Make sure the rear chain is tensioned properly so it doesn't jerk around. The clutch should engage and disengage smoothly, too. Power delivery to the rear tire's contact point must be positive and smooth.

How about Tires

Just think: your motorcycle's capacity to perform on all kinds of surfaces depends on just two small patches of rubber. A sobering thought.

It's easy to comprehend how important the right tread is for maintaining traction on different surfaces. Modern high-quality tires contain special high-hysteresis, or "cling," rubber compounds that provide as much as twenty percent more road adhesion than conventional rubber compounds. Such tires maintain better contact with the road, because they absorb impacts instead of bouncing.

Some tires are harder than others. Although harder tires give longer wear, they don't yield as much traction as softer ones. If you do a lot of long-distance riding in inclement weather, you should opt for the softer tires for the added wet-road grip they provide. For extra traction on wet surfaces, lower tire pressures fifteen to twenty percent. But be sure to inflate them to normal pressure when traveling on dry surfaces.

As for tread design, not only is it important for a street tire to have as much rubber in contact with the road as possible, but the tread pattern must grip the road well, both when upright and when banked.

The tread must shear through water and dirt during wet weather and carry it from underneath the tire by a maze of grooves. And it must do it in a critically short time. If the tread is worn sufficiently, it can't disperse the water effectively. Skidding and hydroplaning can then occur.

Street bikes employ two basic tire designs: the ribbed-tread pattern, strictly a front tire; and the universal type, mounted on either the front or rear.

The ribbed design is ideal for a front tire, because it permits light steering and good road holding during turns. Its circumferential-rib construction prevents slipping when cornering on a wet surface. The ribbed tire isn't subject to irregular wear as other types, and it lasts longer than a block-tread-pattern tire. However, the ribbed design shouldn't be used as a rear tire, as its lack of block treads make it spin under power.

The universal-tread design can be used as a front tire with good results. In some cases, though, it has a tendency to "cup" or wear unevenly. There are many styles of universal tires, but they all feature a block-or triangular-design-tread pattern.

(Left) The ribbed-tread design is used for the front tire where it provides light steering, low rolling resistance, and slip resistance in turns. (Right) The universal-tread pattern can be used on either the front or rear. Both the ribbed and universal designs are intended for the street. *(Courtesy Goodyear Tire Co.)*

Besides the myriad grooves in the tread, there are slits, or "sipes," in the tread itself. They make the tread more flexible and tractional on a wet surface.

For riding both on and off the road, a trials-universal design is recommended. This type features blocks that are more widely spaced than the universal design. A trials tire won't provide quite the same grip on a wet road as will the other two types mentioned. Vigorous cornering isn't recommended with a trials tires, either. But it can be used on either front or back. Some riders put a universal or ribbed on the front and a trials on the back. This setup allows sharper cornering. In the event of too sharp a bank angle, the rear trials tire will break traction first and still give the cyclist a chance to restabilize.

The best off-road tire is a full-knobby design. It's not recommended for serious road riding, because its widely spaced knobs don't present an adequate contact patch to ensure optimal traction on a paved surface. Even on a dry surface, it'll skid more readily in a turn or when braked hard. Other disadvantages are its tendency to vibrate and to wear faster.

Road tires will have tread running up their sidewalls more so than dirt tires. The reason for this is road tires are banked farther for turns, so they must provide more grip during hard-cornering situations.

Highway Hypnosis

Whether you're cautiously feeling your way over a wet road or zipping along a freeway, stay as relaxed as possible without losing touch with your bike's feedback, both from itself and from the road. You want to "feel" what's going on; yet, you don't want to be overly tense so that you fatigue quickly and numb that sensitive link between you and your bike.

You can become too relaxed, however, and dull your senses, leading to "highway hypnosis."

If you ride long distances at a stretch, highway hypnosis can set in. In effect, you then operate your two-wheeler unconsciously.

Highway hypnosis has several causes. The sameness of scenery as you cruise mile upon mile helps to dull your alterness. Then, there's the constant battering of air on your body at high speeds. Moreover, if you don't keep your eyes flicking from point to point, they'll tend to fix on one small area at a time. The hum of the exhaust mixing with the roar of the airstream enhances highway hypnosis even more.

The more your senses become dulled, the more you think about things not related to the job at hand: keeping your motorcycle on the road and not in somebody's trunk.

A peculiarity of highway hypnosis is that it can lead you to gradually increase speed, until you're going faster than you should. Unless you regain your alertness you may wind up in a ditch or ramming the back of a slow-moving truck.

To keep from being highway hypnotized, you've got to mentally (maybe physically) slap yourself at times. Highway hypnosis creeps up on you. Sometimes even fresh air can contribute to it. So, if you're riding extended distances, take a brief break from time to time. Walk around, jump up and down, or take a catnap.

The worst you can do is to keep riding, if you can't keep your mind on it.

Blowouts, Speed Wobbles, and Spills

Most cyclists will ride a lifetime and never experience a blowout or a speed wobble. A spill is something else. Anyway, let's see how to cope with a blowout first.

A blowout in the rear tire will make the rear end of the bike wobble. Shut the throttle and start downshifting as rapidly as possible. Post slightly, so that the footrests are supporting your weight. *Don't* brake! Head for the berm of the road to keep some vehicle from rearending you.

If the front tire should blow out, use the same procedures

but shift your weight to the rear as you post. It's essential that the front of the bike be made as light as possible.

Regardless of which tire blows, put your weight on the footrests. This will enable the bike to shift around underneath you and not upset your balance, while giving the motorcycle a chance to restabilize itself. Keeping the arms "locked" will help prevent the front end from whipping side to side.

Instead of dramatic blowouts, in most cases a punctured tire results in a slow leak, which, luckily, gives you a better chance to stop the bike under control.

A slow leak in the rear tire will cause the rear end to wander from side to side. If it's the front tire leaking, the steering will become sloppy. To minimize blowouts and leaks, frequently check the tires for small objects imbedded in the tread that can work their way through to the inner tube.

A full-fledged speed wobble (also called a fork wobble) can be an unnerving experience. Thankfully, it's rare. Most speed wobbles end almost as quickly as they start.

In Chapter 4, you read how the motorcycle's mechanical condition can contribute to a speed wobble. But it can also be initiated when the front wheel is disturbed by something. In an attempt to bring the wheel back into line by moving the handlebar, the operator sometimes overcontrols, making the wheel deflect to the other side.

Depending on how severely he overcontrols, and on how many times the fork swings from side to side, gyro precession forces can harmonize with the fork deflections. When that happens, the fork deflections become so intense that the fork may bang violently against the stops.

In some cases, where a severe wobble is starting, slowing the bike down only aggravates things.

Some riders who've experienced this phenomenon say the best technique is to speed up instead of slow down. In this way, the gyro effect of the front wheel is strengthened and will cancel the "head shaking" behavior of the bike. Whether you speed up or slow down, relax as much as possible and keep a firm grip on the handlebar. Grip the gas tank between your knees, and let your arms act as buffers for the handlebar's side-to-side movements.

A spill. The very thought of it sends shivers up any biker's spine. Most spills result in nothing more than a shaking up and the loss of some skin. But the expert rider will do everything in his power to prevent a spill. Now some cyclists have the notion that it's better to lay the bike down voluntarily, if an impact with something seems inevitable. The danger here is that you might trap your leg underneath the bike as it slides. By staying upright, you have a chance, however remote it might be, of avoiding impact at the last instant.

If you should spill from the front tire sliding out first, about all you can do is "step off," roll yourself into a ball, and make like a tumbler. Keep your head tucked down between your shoulders, your arms close to your chest, and your legs drawn up. Flailing arms and legs stand a much better chance to catch on something and break.

If you send the rear tire sliding out from an overly hard application of brake, you might be better off to hold the bike down (assuming your leg isn't underneath it) rather than try to upright it. Releasing the brake and trying to stay upright can fling you over the bike like a shot.

Watch Out for Air Turbulence

Because you and your bike weigh considerably less than other vehicles, air turbulence can pose problems. Trucks can create vacuum pockets or turbulence that can upset your bike's tracking. To minimize these conditions, stay as far as possible away from the lane that large vehicles use. When passing trucks, brace yourself for sudden gusts.

Another danger is crosswind. If you're riding behind a hill or through a tunnel and then come out into the open where a strong wind is blowing at right angles, it may catch you by surprise, causing you to overcontrol.

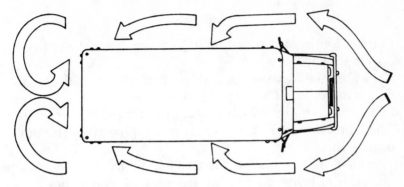

Large vehicles such as trucks and buses pose a threat in the way of creating air turbulence at high speeds. Give them plenty of room.

Watch out for the Bernoulli effect. Large vehicles traveling at high speeds can create a suction effect to pull a motorcycle over into the path of another oncoming vehicle. The Bernoulli effect is compounded if a strong crosswind is blowing from the cyclist's side.

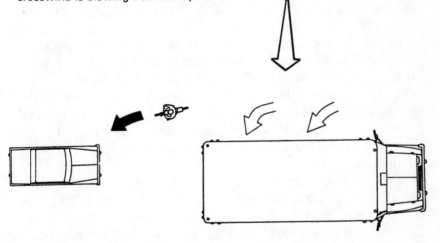

If you're riding in a strong crosswind, slow down. Lean to one side to counteract the crosswind. When you get near a point where the crosswind can't touch you, you'll be prepared to assume normal seating without getting caught by surprise and overreacting to the sudden cessation of crosswind.

Animals

Furry, four-footed creatures add yet another potential threat to your welfare.

Most animals act unpredictably when they're in the vicinity of a motorcycle. The noise and motion of the bike scares them. And at night, the headlight upsets them further. They'll either run back into the woods as you approach or run out in front of you.

Because of their size, deer can be hazardous. They often wait until the last instant to run in front of you. They're one reason it doesn't pay to travel back roads lickety-split. When traveling in heavily wooded areas, get your speed within reason and study the surrounding areas for unusual movements in the grass or for deer standing back near the trees and brush.

If a small animal runs out in front of you and there's no chance to avoid it, brace yourself against the footrests and keep your weight to the rear.

Of all the animals you'll meet, none will be more challenging than man's supposed best friend, old Fido. It's no secret that dogs hate motorcycles. Some dogs just show it more aggressively than others.

Although there are a few dogs mean enough to try and sample your shin, most are cagier than you realize. They'll chase you and bark like crazy, just out of biting distance of your foot.

For the dog who does get uncomfortably close, you might be tempted to poke him with your foot. That's bad. Why? For one reason, you'll upset your bike's balance. For another reason, you might make the dog madder. Then he might quit playing games. Keep your feet on the footrests and speed up to outdistance him. If the dog should confront you head on, prepare for the worst; assume that you're going to hit him.

Bear down on those footrests and shift your weight to the rear. If you should strike him with the front wheel, tug up on the handlebar and gas it, in an effort to lighten the front end.

This technique will give you a better chance to roll on over the dog.

If you ride where there are many bike-chasing dogs, try carrying a water pistol with a solution of ten percent ammonia and ninety percent water. When a dog battles with you, give him a squirt in the eyes. It'll cause only temporary discomfort. What's more, it may cure him of chasing other motorcycles.

Carrying a Passenger

Part of the appeal of motorcycling is sharing it with others. One way of sharing is to carry a passenger. But considering that the combined weight of passenger and operator may equal or surpass the weight of a small motorcycle, stability becomes a problem.

You should have an adequately powered motorcycle to carry double. It should be able to maintain normal highway cruising speeds, and, more importantly, should have reserve power for emergency situations. The bike must have passenger footrests and a grab rail or seat strap. Carrying a passenger on a bike not intended for such a thing means that there won't be any *safe* place for him or her to put his or her feet and to hold on.

Without any means to brace himself or herself during acceleration, cornering, and braking, the passenger is thrown off balance and thereby interferes with your control.

It's particularly important that your passenger sit as far forward as possible to keep the combined bodies' CG as close to the motorcycle's CG as possible. Having the bodies' weight too far rearward will make the front end of the machine light and unstable. Under hard acceleration or during cornering, the bike will be difficult to handle.

Tell your passenger to keep his or her feet on the footrests at all times. A passenger dragging a foot will unbalance the bike. Even when stopped for a red light, the passenger should keep his or her feet on the footrests.

For maximum control when carrying double, your passenger should hold onto your waist. If possible, he or she should interlock fingers.

It's also important to have the passenger lean with you during a turn. A sure way to upset tracking is to have the passenger lean in the opposite direction of bank. If your motorcycle is small and the seat not that roomy, have your passenger hold on by putting his or her arms around your waist and interlocking his or her fingers. This method will make it easier for the passenger to lean with the bike and keep him or her from shifting around unnecessarily.

If it's your passenger's first ride, tell him or her how to hold on and lean with the bike, and take it easy. Don't show off. Refrain from banking turns at steep angles. A first-time passenger will usually resist leaning with the bike. Brace yourself for any sudden movements by the passenger when you corner.

Remember, too, that when carrying double, your control is never as effective as when riding solo. Take that into account.

How to Ride in a Group

A group of motorcyclists riding down the highway in formation is impressive. But there's nothing impressive about a bunch of bikers riding together without organization.

What's the purpose of formation riding? Well, as pleasing as it may be to look at, its real purpose is to enable a group of motorcyclists to travel together safely.

That's the reason the police will stop a bunch of bikers running down the highway in a disorganized fashion, especially if they're too close together. If the lead bike were to go down, other ones following closely behind could pile into it.

The stagger formation positions each bike so that it's a safe distance behind the motorcycle that it's following. Don't stagger bikes when the road is very narrow and winding. Here, the single-file formation is safer. Although formation riding involves many motorcycles at times, in dense traffic conditions, it's safer to divide a large group into smaller sections.

Groups of five to six motorcycles spaced approximately a quarter-mile apart is advisable. Furthermore, each group should have a road captain, or leader, and an assistant road captain, who brings up the rear of the group.

The road captain should place himself to the left side of the lane so that he will have a favorable view of traffic. The second motorcycle is placed to the right rear of the road captain; the third bike is placed to the left rear of the second bike, and so on.

Even with the single-file, the bikes should be slightly staggered to give each rider a view of what's going on up front.

The spacing between the motorcycles depends on the cruising speed of the group and on traffic conditions. The key man

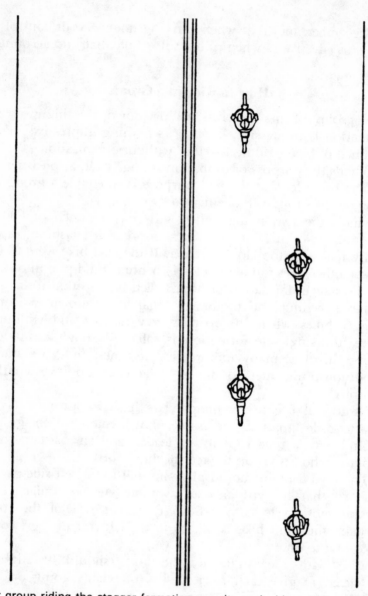

For group riding the stagger formation permits each rider a better view of the road ahead and allows for extra maneuvering room in the event of a mishap.

in a group is the number-two rider. It's his job to establish the proper spacing for all the other riders.

The number-two rider has the added responsibility of compensating for any variations in speed that the road captain causes.

The assistant road captain does more than just tag along after the group. He must act as the overseer of the group and keep any members of the group from lagging behind. He also helps to set up lane-change maneuvers by anticipating the road captain's signals. The assistant road captain usually rides near the center of the lane, where his view of the road captain isn't obstructed by the other bikes.

Hand signals are used to communicate which maneuvers to perform. As the road captain gives a signal, it is passed back from rider to rider until each member has executed the signal.

For example, when the road captain wishes to stop or warn the other riders, he'll extend his left hand down to the side with the palm facing rearward. To slow down, he'll use either hand with a downward "patting" motion. To close up the formation, he'll rotate his hand with an underhand, frontward motion. Conversely, to spread them out, he'll reverse the rotation of his hand as a warning to have them move back. For safety, it's important that the road captain's signal be passed down the line.

If the road captain wants to shift lanes, he'll first give an execution signal. Supposing he wants to shift to the left, he'll extend his left arm out to the left, then bring it back to his chest, as in giving a left-turn signal, then he'll extend it quickly again. If it's a right-lane change, he'll give the standard right-turn signal with his left hand and quickly thrust that hand over to the right side.

Should the road captain wish to cancel any signal, he'll extend his arm down and out to the side and make a waving, "no no" gesture.

Because turn signals are used in conjunction with hand signals, a rider may have forgotten to cancel his turn signal

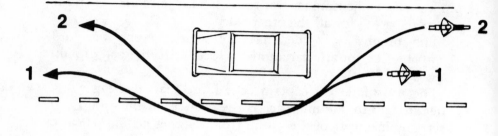

After each cyclist overtakes another vehicle, he should resume his original formation position as soon as possible.

after making a turn or lane change. In that case, an informing rider will extend his arm down and out and close and open his hand to inform the other rider that his turn signal is still blinking.

When passing other vehicle(s), each motorcycle passes in single file. After the group has passed the other vehicle(s) and moved back into their normal traveling lane, they'll resume a stagger formation.

If your group riding is limited to just you and a buddy, you'll probably ride alongside each other. This formation is to be discouraged, unless you are familiar with each other's riding style.

If you belong to a motorcycle club that does extensive group riding, make sure each member thoroughly understands the signals. Additional information can be had from the American Motorcycle Association. If your group doesn't want to abide by standard hand signals as used by the AMA, devise your own. But make sure that each member understands what signals to use. A mixup on the road can be deadly.

10

Defensive Riding Versus the "Other Guy"

In this chapter, you're going to learn how to become something of a two-wheeling psychologist. You're going to take an analytical look at the "other guy" to see what makes him such an unpredictable hazard for you.

First off, let's define the "other guy." Who is he or she? The "other guy" can be a drunk motorist trying to run you off the road, a little old lady stepping into your path, or a child darting at your motorcycle from between two parked cars. Whatever sex or age the "other guy" is, *physically* avoid him. In most cases he won't be looking out for you; so you must be looking out for him.

How Other Drivers React to Motorcycles

Because motorcycles are relatively small and outnumbered by other vehicles, many motorists tend to forget that two-wheelers exist. Even if they're aware of motorcycles, many drivers are still reluctant to share the roads. Why?

Motorcycles tend to upset other drivers. Take, for instance, the cyclist who operates his bike erratically. If he weaves back and forth and constantly changes speed, he soon grates on the nerves of drivers nearby. If his bike has a loud exhaust system, the noise adds to the irritation further. Such a cyclist not only exposes himself to danger, but others as well. So an important aspect of defensive riding is to not ride erratically and make excessive noise.

Inexperienced or elderly motorists, are especially prone to react nervously to motorcycles. You may even have the misfortune to encounter some aggressive, motorcyle-hating driver who'll deliberately try to run you off the road.

The need for defensive riding stems from two primary considerations: (1) Other drivers may not notice you; (2) if and when they do notice you, they may still do something to involve you in an accident. Because the failure of other drivers to notice you is the primary reason for defensive motorcycling techniques, let's begin there.

Mental Set

"I never saw him."

Such a statement is usually made by a driver who has just pulled in front of or into some hapless motorcyclist. The driver probably isn't lying. Such a driver may have good vision and look directly at a motorcycle—*and not even see it.*

This inability to consciously recognize certain objects is a form of mental blindness. When you realize that seeing involves ninety percent mental effort, you can better understand why some people suffer from this unawareness of certain objects.

Psychologists have labeled this condition as Mental Set. Where vehicles are concerned, it means that there are some people who fail to consciously recognize any vehicle smaller than their own. You and your bike don't exist to a driver with Mental Set.

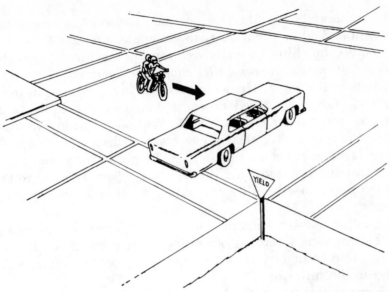

The classic "T" crash. A car pulls in front of—or into—a motorcyclist.

This condition can be caused or enhanced by a preoccupied driver. If you're not careful, *you* can pay dearly for his preoccupation.

Mental Set can lead to the infamous "T" crash, whereby a vehicle pulls out in front of or into a motorcycle.

Intersections: Classic Hazards for Motorcyclists

Let's say that you're riding down the street, and you see a car sitting at a side-street stop sign. As you approach, you see that the driver is looking directly at you. Do you assume that he really does see you? If you do and don't slow down or plan any last-instant evasive action, you're risking your life. What if he has Mental Set?

On top of that, he may be trying to listen to his wife, mother-in-law, six kids, and the ball game on the radio all at the same time. As if that's not bad enough to disrupt him, a girl in shorts across the street at the bus stop has caught his attention. And he's in a hurry to get home, anyway.

So, do you think he really sees you approaching? Maybe he does. *But there's an even better chance he doesn't.*

Assume the worst. He doesn't see you and pulls out in front of you. Get your speed down so you can stop quickly or execute some other evasive action. Without exposing yourself to oncoming traffic, then move over to the extreme side of your lane, *opposite the side he's on.* By positioning yourself to the extreme opposite side of the road where he's at, you're providing yourself with a few extra feet of vital maneuvering space.

Another classic example of the "T" crash occurring at intersections is where an oncoming vehicle makes a left turn directly in front of you. Again, get your speed down, and get over to the curb side.

Some skilled riders use the "cut a donut" technique to evade vehicles that suddenly pull in front of them. It's done by hitting the rear brake and sliding the rear end of the machine around in a "donut." The motorcycle must be leaned slightly to the side, as the rear brake is applied hard. This technique can be performed safely if your speed is kept below thirty-five miles per hour.

Even if other drivers in the situations we've just covered do see you, they might have another mental affliction: indecisiveness.

The guy who sees you coming might be thinking, "Should I pull out now or wait?" He engages in a mental tug of war with his judgment. For some inexplicable reason, at the last instant, he may pull out from that stop sign or make a left turn.

Try to put yourself in his shoes. An approaching motorcycle, because of its smallness, is often difficult to judge regarding speed and distance.

If you speed up or slow down as you approach a driver, you're impairing his judgment further. And if the other vehicle is creeping forward as you get nearer, its driver might make his move in hopes that he still has enough time.

An important part of safely negotiating intersections is to get the other guy's attention. Having the headlight on is an excellent attention getter in daylight. Also, make use of the horn. If your bike doesn't have a loud one, put one on. And wear bright clothing. A fluorescent orange helmet, jacket, or vest will help you to stand out. Wear the brightest, gaudiest clothing you can find. You're not out to look stylish; you're out to increase your chances of survival.

To reduce your reaction time and stopping distance in the event of an emergency, keep your braking foot poised over the rear-brake pedal. And keep your fingers resting lightly on the front-brake lever.

Intersections also pose a danger for the cyclist following a car that is signaling for a turn. The expert cyclist knows that just because the other guy is signaling for a turn, that doesn't mean he'll turn in that direction.

Always stay behind a turn-signaling vehicle until its driver commits himself to turning. If you can see through the rear window, try to discern in which direction he's turning the steering wheel. Unless his front wheels are pointing toward the turn side and he's stopped, wait a few seconds behind the other guy. Even then, there are drivers who can have a change of mind.

Remember: the other guy is unpredictable.

Let's see how to approach an intersection where you have to stop. Where there's more than one lane of traffic going in the same direction, you might be tempted to ride between the two lines of cars, to get ahead of the pack. This practice is to be discouraged, because there's always a good chance you'll get "sandwiched" between two cars.

Also, don't ride too close to a line of parked cars, for there's always someone intent on getting out of his car. Running into a car door suddenly thrust open is a rather unpleasant way to come to a halt.

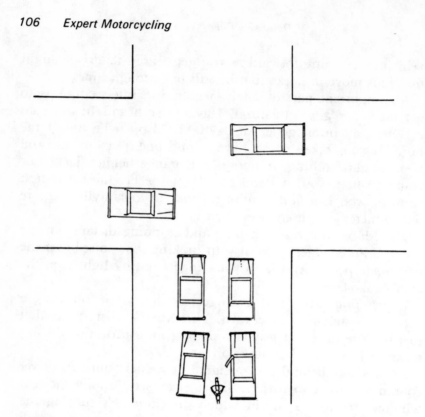

Sneaking up between two lines of vehicles, either moving or stopped, is a good way to get sandwiched or to run into an open car door.

Besides doors being flung open unexpectedly, there's always the danger of a vehicle suddenly pulling away from the curb. For that reason look for vehicles that have their front wheels toward the traffic side and someone sitting behind the wheel. Maybe he's only sitting there waiting for someone and has no intention of pulling out. Then, too, maybe he's ready to swing out, *but doesn't see you coming.* Play it safe and motion for him to pull away.

Also watch out for vehicles backing out of driveways and loading areas of businesses.

When you stop, decelerate with both brakes and downshift.

Keep an eye out for any vehicle behind you that may not be slowing down. Here's the advantage of a mirror. Should you stop suddenly to avoid running a red light, the vehicle behind you might not be able to stop in time. In that case, pull over to the curb as far as you can to give the other driver escape space.

If there's no traffic coming to your right or left, you can accelerate across the intersection or scoot around the corner to avoid being rear ended.

Okay, so what do you do if you're waiting behind another vehicle at a red light and some tractor trailer comes bearing down on you from behind? You can't go forward. But if you lay the bike over to the side slightly and gas it, you can jump the curb or swing out toward the other lane (if there's no other traffic).

So, whenever you pull behind another vehicle at a stop, always leave a little room in front of you for an escape.

While waiting for a light to change, if traffic behind you is stopped, keep the transmission in neutral and the clutch lever out (with the fingers resting on it, just in case you have to pop into gear quickly). Don't sit there with the bike in gear, idly revving the engine. It's possible that the clutch cable could be weak and snap at an inopportune time. Or the end fitting could come off, while you have the clutch lever pulled in. And if you're in gear with the engine revved up at the time the cable lets go, guess where you're going? Yep. Right into someone's trunk, or across the intersection into—or in front of—another vehicle.

If you do sit there with the bike in gear, apply the front or rear brake. This is just a precautionary action in case the clutch cable should let go. You never know.

When the light changes to green, hesitate for two or three seconds before you pull out—to make sure there's not some joker trying to crash the light. Waiting those few seconds will prevent you from hitting a light-crashing pedestrian, too. Be careful around elderly people and small children—and not just at intersections. They may be hard of hearing and hard of seeing, which makes them vulnerable to getting struck by vehicles. Watch out for small children who may suddenly try to run across the street or zip out from between parked cars to retrieve a ball.

When turning at intersections, don't overlook signaling. Your avoiding contact with the other guy depends on how effectively you can communicate your hand signals and/or turn signals. Indicate a left turn by extending your left arm straight out to the side. For a right turn, raise the left arm up to the side and bend your elbow so the forearm is pointing toward the right side. To warn the driver behind you that you're slowing down, extend your left arm down to the side. If you're carrying a passenger and want to keep your hands on the grips, have him or her do the signaling for you. Just be sure that your passenger gives the proper signal when you want it.

Escape Space

Whether you're waiting for a light to change, riding down the street, or out on the highway, always be on the lookout for escape space. Imagine situations where you'll have to effect evasive action to escape danger. Visualize how you'll maneuver your bike and where you'll go to avoid trouble. With practice, you will react much more quickly and accurately to dangerous situations.

But if you never program your mind beforehand as to how you'll react to an emergency, and you're then confronted with one, you can freeze. Maybe you'll never react exactly the way you visualize you will, but your mind will have some valuable data to go on.

Defensive Riding on the Open Road

Out on the open road, you still have the major problems of town riding, namely that of coping with other drivers' unpredictable behavior. But these problems are intensified by the

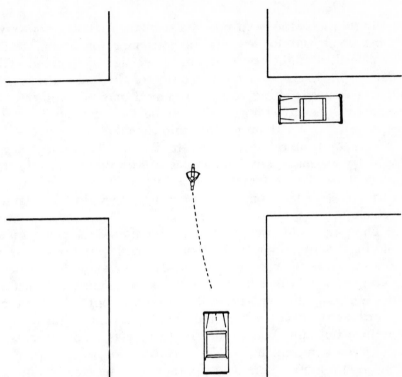

When negotiating an intersection, allow for escape space between you and another vehicle waiting at a side-street stop sign.

higher speeds on the open road. And, sadly, many drivers don't have their perception and judgment geared to the high speeds they drive.

You've often heard the expression "being in the right place at the right time," haven't you? Well, it has a special meaning when you're occupying part of the road. Previously you read that the center portion of the lane is often the slipperiest. That leaves the outer areas on which to ride. And here's where there are two different views on the subject: some riders say it's best to stay on the right side near the berm (if it's a two-lane highway), and others say the left side of the lane is the safest. There's something to be said for both.

By riding on the berm side of a two-lane highway, you leave more room on the left side of your lane for an oncoming vehicle that might veer over onto your side of the road. The danger with riding on the berm side of the lane, however, is that a vehicle passing you from behind may not pull out far enough. The driver may feel that he has adequate room to squeeze by you without pulling into the other lane.

Even by your riding on the left side of the lane, that same vehicle can snag your bike as it swings around you into the other lane. Don't forget that a lot of drivers don't space themselves as far from a motorcycle as they do for a larger vehicle.

Then again, by occupying the right side of the lane, you're placing yourself in a blind spot of vehicles in front of you. For that reason, when you get ready to pass another vehicle, swing over to the left side of the lane momentarily before pulling out. This will allow the driver in front of you to pick your bike up in his mirror and possibly restrain himself from pulling out into you as he, in turn, gets ready to pass a slower-moving vehicle.

Forgetting about the oil drippings for a moment, riding in the center of the lane has another drawback. If you're following another vehicle closely, you might not see something on the road that the other vehicle manages to pass over.

Where there are multi-lane freeways, ride in the lane that has traffic traveling within your bike's normal cruising speed. If you ride in one of the middle lanes, you'll have to monitor traffic on both sides. Mirrors will be a big help, but you'll still have to frequently flick glances over *both* shoulders to check those rear-side areas, which are potential blind spots.

How closely should you follow another vehicle, anyway? The expert rider will allow himself at least a three-second trailing distance behind a vehicle. To determine that distance, when the driver ahead of you passes a tree, pole, or some other object nearby, you shouldn't reach that point until three seconds later.

When it comes to passing other vehicles, there's an old saying: "When in doubt, *don't.*" In other words, if you're not sure you can get around other vehicles safely, don't risk it. Passing other vehicles can be hair-raising, especially if you're riding a relatively underpowered machine and/or carrying a passenger or luggage.

When you're ready to pass on a two- or three-lane road, get over to the left side of your lane so you'll have a good view of the road ahead. Study both the road ahead, and, if you can see through his rear window, the driver ahead of you. Look for obstacles on the road, oncoming vehicles moving erratically, vehicles on the left berm side that could suddenly move onto the road as you pass, anything that can interfere with your passing safely.

If you can observe the driver in front of you, note his actions. Is he talking to a passenger and not concentrating on his driving? Is he moving his head from side to side, as though he's looking for a place to turn off?

Study other drivers' behavior. Often they'll tip you off that they're about to do something. Don't wait for the other vehicle's brake lights to go on to show that the driver's slowing down; they might not be functioning. The same goes for turn signals.

Before you start to pass, signal to the driver in front of you. If your headlight is on, flip the high/low beam switch. Or put your turn signal on,. and signal with your extended left arm. Make that other driver aware that you're about to pass.

If everything looks okay to pass, downshift, if necessary, so you can obtain optimum acceleration. Don't try to pass in high gear. And travel an arc wide enough so that you'll be able to pull back into your regular lane without cutting directly in front of the passed vehicle. Yet, the arc shouldn't be too wide so that you stay out in the passing lane too long. When you're ready to cut back in, signal. Then glance into your mirror, or better yet, look over your right shoulder to see where the vehicle is you've just passed. Sometimes as you pass someone, he'll accelerate. If you don't check for him, you may end up turning into the side of his vehicle.

Be Courteous to Others

Be courteous to the other guy. Why?

Many people still think of motorcyclists as holdovers from the Wild One era of the 1950s. The last thing they expect is for some cyclist to give them the right of way.

Fool them. Look at it this way: if you don't give the other guy the right of way, he may take it anyway—at your expense. Besides, it won't take that much of your time to let the other guy have the right of way.

Good deeds have a way of repaying themselves. That courtesy you extend to a motorist now may make him look favorably upon motorcyclists in the future. Maybe he'll give some other rider the right of way later.

Who knows, it might even prevent an accident.

11

After the Sun Goes Down

There's a certain mystique about riding a motorcycle at night. As its cyclopean headlight probes the road ahead, the two-wheeler seems to float through another dimension. However enchanting motorcycling at night may be, it nonetheless presents hazards.

Actually, the hazards you have at night are the same ones you face during daylight. But they're intensified by your inability to see them *as well* at night. Your vulnerability is further enhanced by the fact that the other guy can't see as well, either. Drivers squinting through dirty windshields, slippery spots lying on the road unnoticed, and suicidal animals running in front of you—all tend to make night riding demanding.

To realize what you're up against, consider these startling facts. You lose *eighty percent or more* of your visual perception at night. And if your vision is only 20/40, your sight is reduced by ten times that of a person with 20/20 sight. Even if your vision is 20/20, your sight is diminished by nearly ninety percent of your daytime capacity. Besides impaired perception and the inability to fully distinguish contrast, your depth perception and judgment of speed and distance suffer, too.

When you look at those facts, you might wonder why anyone would venture out at night on a motorcycle.

Yet, the human eye and mind have the capacity to compensate somewhat for visual shortcomings. As with learning to see better in daylight, you can improve your night vision.

Night Sight

To see better at night, you should have some idea how the eye functions in darkness. In daylight, the central portion of the retina provides the sharpest field of view, due to its high concentration of light sensors called *cones*. Therefore, you see more clearly when you look directly at something. At night, however, this central area becomes a blind spot, because the cones are relatively insensitive to darkness.

To see something better in darkness requires that low-light sensors, *rods*, be used. They're located in the peripheral areas of the retina. Turning the head slightly to one side allows the rods to "line up" on an object so that it can be viewed more clearly.

You can prove this phenomenon to yourself. Look directly at a cluster of lights in the distance or at a group of stars. Then turn your head a few degrees to one side. Notice which way enables you to see more lights clearly.

Furthermore, by observing your surroundings, you'll pick up more objects in greater detail.

But the danger with trying to see more clearly at night is that it's not hard to strain your eyes. And when you strain to see, you place the eyes under tension so that they see less than if you made no effort. The idea is to be interested in what you're looking at, without straining your eyes to see it.

Because seeing is mostly a mental process (the brain interprets the images the eyes pick up), eye strain quickly leads to fatigue and inattentiveness. At night these conditions can occur more quickly, due to reduced visibility.

The eyes thrive on mobility; they must be kept moving. As soon as you stare at one point for more than three seconds, you tend to become slower reacting. When you ride along, don't stare at distant lights, reflectors on guard rails, or oncoming headlights. They all have hypnotic influence. Instead, use quick eye movements, with the head immobile. If you keep the eyes fixed and move only your head, your field of view will blur.

Blinking helps relieve tension in the eyes and helps them to see more. As simple as it is, frequent closing of the eyelids provides momentary rest for the eyes. Blinking also helps to keep the eyeballs moist, which reflects excessive glare from oncoming headlights. Every so often, close your eyelids tightly for an instant to increase circulation and to minimize fatigue.

Some people suffer from a depth-perception defect regarding the color red called protanopia. This condition makes the color red seem farther away than it really is. So, a protanopic driver is more apt to run into the back of a vehicle at night. The single taillight on a motorcycle is difficult for a protanopic driver to notice.

Imagine what you're up against if the guy behind you has both Mental Set and protanopia.

Monitor the traffic behind you. Keep an eye on those mirrors. If someone gets too close for comfort, pull off the road and let him by.

If your bike has a small taillight, mount a larger one on it. To warn a driver that he's too close to your bike, pump the brake to take advantage of the extra brightness of the brake light.

Wear white or light-reflective clothing at night. If your bike doesn't have turn signals, wear white gloves, or put reflective tape on darker gloves so that other drivers can see you give signals.

Riding in fog can quickly disorient you to the point that you can run off the road before you know what's happened. To minimize the disorienting effects of fog, get your speed down and flick your headlight on low beam. High beam will bounce off the fog and provide less visibility than low beam. Your eye protection will load up frequently with moisture, so you'll have to wipe it clean.

And keep those eyes flicking about. It's easy to stare off into the fog in one direction, hoping to get a glimpse of something. Fog has such a hypnotic effect that some cyclists and drivers get dizzy if they ride in it for long.

How to Avoid Headlight Glare from Other Vehicles

One of the annoyances of night riding is that of other vehicles' headlights. A string of oncoming vehicles, especially those on high beam, can produce enough glare to strain your vision. What's more, looking at a constant stream of headlights makes it harder for the eyes to adapt to the surrounding darkness. If you stare at those headlights for long, you know what can happen.

You must avoid looking directly at headlights, but you still must keep track of those other vehicles, in case one of them crosses into your lane. Moreover, you need to keep track of *your* position, too. To do all this, use a simple technique called the three-point focusing system. What you do is scan a triangular pattern by briefly looking at three different points on the road. By using quick eye movements, first glance at a point on your right, directly opposite the approaching vehicle. Then shift your sight to a point on the road near the vehicle, then back to a spot a short distance in front of your bike. By repeated eye scanning, headlight glare is minimized, while you maintain your position on the road and keep track of other vehicles, too.

A variation of that system is the two-point focusing system in which your sight is first directed to a point on the road alongside the other vehicle and then back to a point in front of your bike. Every so often, glance to the right side of your lane to see if you're maintaining position.

Some cyclists alternate closing and opening each eye so that only one eye is open at a time. Although this method permits each eye to rest briefly, it eliminates peripheral vision on the side of the closed eye. And if another vehicle or an animal were to suddenly come onto your closed-eye side of the road, you might not notice it in time.

Don't make the mistake of wearing tinted glasses or faceshields at night to reduce headlight glare. Although they help in that respect, they severely curtail vision. The only benefit of tinted eyewear at night is that of wearing sunglasses inside a brightly lighted restaurant or some other illuminated place. When you go out into the dark later, your eyes don't have to undergo such a harsh adjustment to the darkness. If you don't protect your eyes from the brightness inside, it can take up to half an hour for them to fully adjust to the darkness later. Even if you wear sunglasses inside, still give your eyes a few minutes to adjust to the darkness once outside. Travel at a moderate speed and be extra alert.

If your plastic eyewear is badly scratched, oncoming headlights will be more irritating and blinding. And if there's enough moisture in the air to gather on the lens or faceshield, this irritation and "blindness" will be worse. During daylight you won't notice scratched eyewear as much. But at night, it refracts light rays, causing this irritation and "blindness."

Should you ever get blinded by headlights, slow down and pull over to the side of the road. But be careful when you slow down. If there's someone behind you, he may be blinded, too, and not see you slowing down.

Believe it or not, oncoming headlight beams do have some advantages. The "sidesweep" effect of headlights, which is the lateral spread of the beams, can reveal poor surface conditions, especially wet surfaces. Learn how to make use of ambient lighting from street lights, store windows, billboards, etc., which reflect light on the road.

Headlights provide an additional advantage in that they can

reveal the presence of another vehicle before you see it. For instance, when a vehicle is on the other side of a hill or is coming around a blind curve, its headlights will reflect off the underside of telephone cables or off tree foliage. You can warn other drivers of your presence by flicking your high/low beam. There's a good chance they'll notice your headlight beam flickering off the cables or trees.

Passing Other Vehicles

There's a way to communicate to another driver that you're about to pass around him.

As you come up on a slower-moving vehicle, flip your high/low beam a couple of times to signal your intentions. If your bike has turn signals, signal for a left turn, so the driver can see in his mirror that you intend to pull around him. Then pull out in a flat arc, and when you're alongside him, flip to high beam to light up the road ahead. If there's oncoming traffic, you won't be able to flip to high beam for fear of blinding other drivers. But if there's no immediate oncoming traffic, flip to high beam. The other driver may respond by flipping his lights to high beam to provide additional illumination of the road ahead. When it's safe for you to pull back in, he'll "say" so by flipping his lights back to low beam. Truck drivers are noted for using their lights to communicate to other drivers.

Animals

It can be difficult to notice animals alongside the road at night. But deer will reveal their presence by their eyes, which will look like the ends of shiny cans suspended in the air. Deer are more unpredictable at night, because the headlights confuse them.

When riding in rural areas, scan the sides of the road for movement in the brush or for those shiny spots hanging in the air. If a deer does run in front of you, watch it! There's usually at least one more close behind.

Your Physical Condition

Would you believe there are certain substances you can ingest that will effect your night vision?

You should already know what effect alcohol has on your vision. But did you know that even tobacco and certain ordinary drugs can severely limit your vision and judgment at night?

Take tobacco. With smoking there's always carbon monoxide produced by the incomplete combustion of the tobacco. The carbon monoxide interferes with the body's intake and distribution of oxygen. Because blood has an affinity 200 times greater for carbon monoxide than for oxygen, there are fewer blood cells available for the absorption of oxygen.

You don't even have to smoke to absorb large amounts of carbon monoxide. You absorb it just by riding in heavy traffic.

Without adequate oxygen, you suffer impairment of not only your sight, but your reflexes, coordination, depth perception, and judgment, too.

Let's get back to alcohol, since that seems to be the real road troublemaker. The danger of alcohol is that it's immediately absorbed into the bloodstream. Although some people can tolerate more alcohol than others, it takes only *one* ounce of alcohol to appreciably effect your driving or riding skills. For most people the critical level is .08 percent of alcohol. Two whiskies in an hour will reach this figure. Besides alcohol's already mentioned bad effects, it also induces a condition known as "tunnel vision." What happens here is that the peripheral vision decreases until a person sees only a narrow area.

The guy who has been drinking poses a real threat to your welfare. Often a driver who has been heavily drinking won't handle a car much differently from anyone else. But if an emergency arises, he won't have full control. A good rule to go by is that *every* driver at night is under the influence of alcohol. Of course, this isn't true, but it'll put you on the defensive and give you a better chance to react to other drivers.

Alcohol and tobacco aren't the only substances that can dull your faculties. Even the ingredients found in common medicines used in treating colds, headaches, and other everyday ailments can effect your alertness.

Remember: you don't have the margin for error at night that you have during daylight. Watch what you ingest before riding at night.

Bike Preparation

If you're going to ride safely at night, your bike's lighting system must be in good working order. You certainly don't want to have your lights to go out when rolling down a busy highway or when banking a sharp turn.

Take the headlight. If it's not set right, it won't light up the right portions of the road. If it's off just one degree, sideways or up or down, it'll lose about thirty percent of its effectiveness. And it'll lose even more than that if there's a film of dirt and bugs on it. When adjusting the headlight, make sure you're sitting on the bike with the tires inflated correctly.

Check your owner's manual for specific beam-adjustment procedures.

Unless the headlight is a sealed-beam unit, moisture can find its way inside the headlight shell and destroy that mirrorlike finish on the light reflector, which amplifies the light. Don't polish that reflector, either, because it consists of a very thin coating that will easily rub off. You can moisture proof the headlight shell by using a silicone-type sealant around the rim and shell joint.

It's also a good idea to periodically replace the bulbs in the headlight and taillight assemblies. Carry the old bulbs for spares by taping them inside the headlight shell. You never know when a bulb will blow out, because vibration can prematurely break the filaments. If you ever do have a headlight go out, switch quickly to the other beam. It may still be intact and capable of staying that way for quite a while.

A quartz-iodine headlight provides a beam of light over a great distance. Despite the great distances they can cover, however, some lights of this type have a relatively narrow beam. The value of a quartz-iodine light is the way it lights up a road for high-speed driving. But it can be blinding to oncoming drivers, which is why it's illegal in some states.

For heavy-fog conditions, a fog light, mounted low on the bike with the upper portion of its lens masked (to prevent flashback from the fog), is recommended. Unlike the quartz-iodine light, a fog light has a much wider beam and a shorter projection.

Rear illumination is just as important as up front. Thankfully, modern motorcycles are using larger taillights, which helps to keep protanopic drivers from running up rear fenders as much as they used to. If your bike has a small taillight, think about mounting a larger one. As for the brake light, make sure that it goes on without having to depress the brake pedal very far. Some cyclists even hook the rear-brake light up to the front brake.

Before you start modifying your bike's lighting system, check your state laws to see what's legal. Some states have odd laws as to the type and number of lights you can mount. What's more, the *way* you mount them should be checked into, also.

Now, if you use your head and keep your bike in shape for night riding, you can *safely* ride "after the sun goes down."

12

Off the Road

If you're strictly a paved-road enthusiast, you might wonder why anyone in his right mind would want to go bouncing over the countryside. And unless you've ridden across a desert in the early morning hours, followed a trail through the forest, or just chased a rabbit across a field under a blue sky, you might think that off-road riding is only for the motocross and trials riders.

Nothing could be further from the truth.

What Off-Road Riding Offers

Off-road riding has a strong appeal to the average cyclist who just "wants to get away from it all," even if it's only a temporary escape. There's something about getting off by yourself occasionally, amidst nature's surroundings, that can help you "get your head on straight."

If you're the philosophic, introverted type, your bike can

take you to some out-of-the-way place where you can "contemplate your place in the universe." Or you might take to the idea of loading a friend on the back with a picnic lunch and heading out to some shady tree. Or your preference for a day in the dirt might be playing chase with a bunch of your buddies.

Because off-road riding, or dirt riding, is essentially an individual experience (like street riding), you can make it what *you* want.

Your bike is a willing servant, ready to obey your every whim. Climb a hill, follow a path, chase a rabbit—just name it. Then do it!

With a bike fitted for off-road riding, you can search for those idyllic, little-known camping and fishing spots as you seek a respite from the problems of civilization. *(Courtesy Kawasaki Motor Corp.)*

With dirt riding, you don't have to worry about some clod in a two-ton box of steel running up your rear fender. Indeed, dirt riding can be a mind-bending experience, if you develop the enthusiasm for it.

Besides the fun and satisfaction it provides, off-road cycling also enables you to develop expertise with your cycle. The control techniques you learn help you to become a much better rider than if you just stayed on the road. As you traverse different kinds of terrain, you learn how to react instinctively to your bike's movements.

You can't find a better way to sharpen your off-road skills than by trials riding. This form of motorcycling will truly make you feel as though you are part of your bike. *(Courtesy Yamaha International Corp.)*

But as enjoyable and instructive as it is, dirt riding also imposes certain obligations on you. For one, you should never trespass on private property, or make unnecessary noise or disturbances where there are other people close by. And because we must be concerned with ecology today, you should exercise discretion in areas where you can create irreparable harm to the soil and vegetation. Dirt riding doesn't entitle you to wantonly deface nature. You can tread on the terrain and still not damage it.

If you're venturing far off the road to engage in serious off-road work, it's best to do so with a couple of other riders. If you go by yourself and have a bad spill or breakdown, you could be in a hell of a fix.

How to Dirt-Prep Your Bike

If your idea of off-road riding is to make a couple of passes around the local picnic grounds, you won't have to modify your bike to make it more "dirtable." But if you'd like to make your bike more at home in the dirt, there are several modifications you can make.

First, for moderate speed racing over rough ground, a fairly short wheelbase and a high ground clearance are two desirable features. Second, you need to pare any excess weight from your two-wheeler to make it handle easily in the rough stuff. Throwing a heavy bike around soon proves tiring. You can begin your weight reduction by replacing a large-capacity steel gas tank with a smaller one to reduce "top hamper." This term applies to the amount of weight situated above the bike's center of gravity; the lower it is, the less top heavy the bike will be. To keep weight to a minimum, install a gas tank made of fiberglass.

Weight can be further lowered by mounting abbreviated, high-impact plastic fenders. Even the stock lighting system can be replaced with a smaller setup. But don't sacrifice good lighting just to save a few pounds in the dirt.

If you ride by yourself, think about replacing the stock dual seat with a smaller type.

Regardless what else you do to your bike to make it dirtworthy, two of the most important modifications you can make to it concern gearing and tires.

Most street bikes, including those used for dual-purpose riding (street and dirt), are geared too high for off-road use. But with the conventional chain-and-sprocket drives, it's a relatively simple matter to alter overall gearing. You have the option of changing the gearbox sprocket and/or the rear-wheel sprocket to arrive at a lower gearing suitable for off-road.

Arriving at a particular gearing is mostly a trial-and-error process. To give your bike more low-end grunt, you can either put a one-tooth-smaller sprocket on the gearbox or a three-teeth-larger sprocket on the rear wheel. Either sprocket will give you the same result.

If you still don't have the low-end power you want, you may have to go to a gearbox sprocket with two fewer teeth than stock or to a rear-wheel sprocket with six more teeth. Don't go too low because your bike may not have a decent cruising speed later out on the road. Like everything else about a dual-purpose bike, gearing is a compromise at best.

Complementing gearing are tires. For the dual-purpose bike, the trials-universal design is the way to go. It's good for climbing out of ruts and for maintaining lateral stability on soft surfaces. And it's a fairly good road tire, so long as you don't brake or corner too briskly on wet surfaces.

The sports-knobby tire, with its big, widely spaced cleats, is a true off-road tire. It'll provide maximum traction on loose, soft surfaces. But on hard, smooth dirt surfaces, it can perform in a skatelike fashion.

Full-time off-road bikes often use a trials tire on the front with a sports-knobby on the back.

For maximum traction in the dirt, fit the widest tires possible.

Surprisingly, for firm dirt surfaces, even standard road tires

(Left) The trials-universal tread design is a good tire for riding both on and off the road. It can be used either front or back. (Right) For serious riding in the loose stuff, the sports-knobby design will provide optimum traction. It's strictly an off-road tire. *(Courtesy Goodyear Tire Co.)*

offer fairly good traction. The ribbed design on the front, however, can be troublesome in the mud. The areas between the ribs load up with mud, until the tire is so smooth that it hardly permits any traction.

Regardless of the tread design, traction can be improved by dropping tire pressure twenty to thirty percent, depending on the surface. For easier going in rough terrain, a twenty-one-inch front wheel will climb over obstacles easier than an eighteen- or nineteen-inch wheel.

An upswept exhaust system is something else you should consider, unless you have an enduro-type motorcycle. A lighter, smaller exhaust type and muffler located up high helps to lower weight. They're out of the way up there, too.

A skid plate is a must. Without one, it's almost certain that a rock will find its way into the engine's belly.

Don't forget the footrests. Most of the ones on street bikes are rubber covered. But for off-road use, where the feet are more apt to slip off, the footrests should have a serrated steel surface, with the center areas cut away for mud and dirt to fall through from the soles of the footwear. Also, to prevent them from snagging on something, the footrests should be of the folding, spring-loaded type so that if they do hit something, they'll bend back out of the way, and then snap forward once past the obstacle.

Furthermore, the footrests should be repositioned, if necessary, to the rear so that you can shift your weight rearward to maintain better rear-tire traction.

Now for the handlebar. Here is another component that you'll have to compromise on for dual-purpose riding. A fairly low, wide handlebar will yield maximum leverage with which to throw the bike around. High-riser bars with a lot of intricate bends have no place on a dirt bike.

Because an off-road mount should have a tight-turning radius, the fork stops on your street machine might have to be filed or ground off to permit the wheel to turn farther to either side. However, if too much of the stops is taken off, the handlebar might hit the gas tank when it's turned to the full-lock position.

You should definitely have a good air filter. Nothing will wear an engine out more prematurely than dirt and sand it sucks through its carburetor. Almost as bad as having no filter at all is running with one that's all choked up. A dirty filter restricts air so that the intake charge has a higher ratio of gas to air, which dilutes the protective film of lubrication on the cylinder walls and hastens wear.

When you ride in forested areas, make sure the muffler or exhaust pipe has a spark arrester. It only takes one spark to start a fire. So, keep old Smokey the bear smiling: use a good spark arrester.

In some states, it's illegal to modify certain components on a motorcycle licensed for the road. So be sure to look into this matter before you start to alter that streetster for off-road riding.

Despite how well you prep your bike, there always looms the threat of a breakdown in the boondocks. For that reason you should always prepare for mechanical malfunctions. Carry a compact but comprehensive tool kit. To save space, you can take along an adjustable wrench in place of several other size wrenches.

Because chain failure is always a possibility, include a chain-repair kit. Then, too, flat tires aren't unheard of. In place of a tube-repair kit and a tire pump, you might take along a can of compressed air/tube sealer. It's less bulky than the other flat-fixer items mentioned, and a lot quicker to use.

Another good idea is to plastic coat the ignition system to make it waterproof.

Prepare beforehand for all kinds of emergencies. For instance, a piece of wire and a section of nylon rope can come in handy. Use the wire to secure a component in place that has lost its attaching bolt or screw; the rope can tow another inoperable cycle out from the back country.

There are many ways in which you can prepare your machine for the dirt. It all depends to what extent you want to go in for this form of motorcycling. But your bike is only part of it. What about you?

Are You Dirt-Prepped?

As important as it is to get your bike ready for the rough, you've got to prep yourself, too.

Protective clothing is essential, because the chances for a spill are greater off the road than on the road. Climbing hills, dodging rocks, and crossing streams all present traction and control problems that can spill you. But if you're dressed right, dropping in the dirt won't hurt that much.

Naturally, you'll need a good helmet. If you don't have one, park the bike and take a hike instead.

A leather, vinyl, or denim jacket, along with heavy pants, will minimize the chances of brush burn occurring. Heavy footwear and gloves are definitely needed. Footwear should be heavier and higher than that worn for the road. Since your feet can take a real beating from the terrain, steel-toed footwear is recommended. If you ever get your foot wedged in between a rock and your bike, you'll know why it's recommended.

Eye protection is another must. Even at low speeds, a low-hanging branch or a stone-hard insect can hit you in the eye. To keep dust from swirling into your eyes, snug-fitting goggles are still the best protection.

If you go in for high-speed riding over large expanses of ground, think about looking into some of the specialized protective items that motocrossers wear. Chest and face guards, shoulder pads, thigh pads, and heavily padded jackets and

Motocross racing is just one form of off-road racing for the dirt buff. *(Courtesy Yamaha International Corp.)*

pants provide the optimum in body protection. You can never have enough protective garb on when you're sliding on *terra firma*.

Then there's the mental aspects to consider. Maintain a positive attitude so that you feel capable of riding on different surfaces safely, *once you have the basic skills developed.* Don't get too brash and stretch your luck beyond your skills. Temper your attitude with common sense.

But before you do anything, learn the basics. Don't try to run before you can walk.

Getting the Feel of Dirt Riding

To a first-time dirt rider, it can be unnerving to be astride a motorcycle as it slides and wanders around. Your first reaction is to squeeze the grips hard and stiff arm the handlebar movements. But it's only natural for a motorcycle to want to move around a lot on the dirt.

You must learn to let it shift about and "have its head," so to speak. Once you learn not to fight it, you'll come to react instinctively to your bike's behavior without overcontrolling it. You'll maintain better control of your machine by holding the handlebar just firm enough to keep the grips from slipping out of your hands. And don't lock your arms in an effort to stifle the handlebar movements. If you find your arms getting tired, you can take a lot of the tension off them by gripping the gas tank between your knees to help control the motorcycle.

Incidentally, if you plan a serious session in the dirt, first sprinkle talcum powder in your gloves. The powder will reduce friction between your hands and gloves and keep too many blisters from forming.

As with street riding, keep your feet on the footrests as much as possible.

Of course, learning to ride off the road is the same as learning to ride on the road in the sense that you undertake it progressively. But with dirt riding, you have more leeway for

Dangling a foot at high speed across an open expanse is a sure invitation to a broken foot or ankle. Whenever possible, keep both feet on the footrests. *(Courtesy Kawasaki Motor Corp.)*

error, regarding traction. In road riding you try to keep the tires from breaking traction and skidding. But off the road, there are situations where you'll deliberately make the tires skid to effect a certain kind of maneuver. Once you get the hang of skidding your bike around at will, you'll be able to perform maneuvers you never thought possible.

Even your braking technique will vary somewhat from the way you brake on the road. Braking on loose surfaces most of the time requires a deft touch to keep the wheels from locking up and skidding. Off the road, downshifting while applying the brakes is the accepted method, as it is on the road. Furthermore, learn to use the front brake off the road as much as you can without locking up the wheel. But there'll be situations where you can lock up the rear brake to control the bike. One technique is "crossing-up" to make the motorcycle change direction. To learn how, first find a fairly level area where you can accelerate to fifteen to twenty miles per hour. Then lock up the rear wheel by applying hard rear brake.

By leaning slightly to the side opposite the rear brake pedal, you can make the rear end of the bike come around. As it does, put your foot down for support, lay the bike over even farther, and cock the front wheel in the direction that the rear end is sliding. The bike can be leaned over so far as to drag the footrest, which acts as a stabilizer to keep the bike from rolling right on over its side. Once you get the bike over and sliding, don't let it come back up. If it does, it can throw you.

By cocking the front wheel in the direction of the rear-end slide, you keep the motorcycle from spinning around in a circle. The idea of a cross-up is to bring the motorcycle about until it's heading in a new direction, without spinning completely around.

When you've acquired the skill to cross-up at low speeds, progressively increase the speed in five- or ten-mile per hour increments until you get up to thirty-five to forty miles per hour. Once you get to that point, you're ready to start using the throttle to help cross-up the bike. And that means going back to the low speeds you used initially.

You get your bike up to fifteen or twenty miles per hour, jam on the rear brake, and lean the bike over. But now, instead of coming to a dead stop as you did before, you let off the brake and twist the throttle on hard. The rear tire will not only slide out to the side, it'll also turn to make the bike go forward, better enabling you to control the direction in which you want the bike to go.

When you've become proficient at crossing-up the motorcycle in the ways just mentioned, you can go on to learning how to do it with just the throttle. When you get to where you want to change the machine's direction, you nudge the bike over and give it hard throttle to make the rear tire break traction and kick the rear end around.

The cross-up technique is effective whenever you need to quickly maneuver the bike onto a new course but don't have the time to slow down.

A variation of cross-up is used by dirt riders traveling at high speeds. Should an obstacle suddenly appear in your path, snap the throttle shut, then snap it back open. This technique kicks the rear wheel out to one side, which points the front end onto a new heading.

Another technique is "cutting donuts." This maneuver spins the motorcycle around in a circle or series of circles.

To learn how to do it, stop the bike in low gear and put a foot down for support on the side that you want to turn. Then tilt the bike slightly to that side, give it hard throttle, and *hold on!* The machine will chase itself around in a circular fashion. The advantage of this technique is that it allows you to change directions quickly in tight places.

"Cutting donuts" teaches you control on loose surfaces. Lay the bike over, turn the front wheel toward the lean side, turn on the gas, and *hold on!*

These maneuvers mentioned so far are helpful in teaching you to gain better control of your bike in off-balance situations.

To maintain effective control of your bike and to keep your balance, you must learn to ride by standing on the footrests and by employing Body English. In fact, you'll use these two techniques unconsciously most of the time, whether you carefully pick your way over some slippery surface or ride at high speed through some open stretch of desert.

If you're using your street bike for playing in the dirt, you might have to alter the controls so that they feel more comfortable when you're up on the footrests.

At first, it seems awkward to ride over uneven terrain poised on the footrests and "hanging out" to one side to maintain balance.

If you're not familiar with this form of motorcycling, learn it by practicing on a fairly level surface. Then as it becomes natural to operate your bike this way, try it on a more uneven surface.

When you get used to standing on the footrests and shifting your body around, see how tightly you can turn without losing your balance and putting a foot down for support. Experiment by leaning the bike in toward the center of the turn, while you hang out to the outside of the bike and bear down on the outside footrest. Then try the same maneuver by pushing the bike "over" to the outside of the turn, as you lean in toward the center and bear down on the inside footrest.

Another way to learn how to use Body English is to ride in a straight line (at varying speeds) and thrust your weight to one side and the bike to the other side, in an effort to dodge obstacles in your path.

When you become able to ride across rough terrain at high speeds, you'll need to spend a great deal of the time crouched on the footrests. Why? Your legs are natural shock absorbers, and it's easier on them to absorb impact forces than for your spine and internal organs to do so when you're seated. By posting on the footrests and by keeping your weight to the rear, you keep the front end of the bike light, so that front-end impact forces are minimized.

Just before you hit a bump with the front tire, snap the throttle farther open and tug up on the handlebar. If you do this properly, the bike should land rear wheel first after it clears the bump. Whatever you do, don't hit the brakes just before the front tire hits the bump. If you do, the fork legs will compress from weight transference, and the impact forces will be much more severe, due to the heavily loaded front end.

When landing after jumping over an obstacle, keep weight to the rear and tug up on the handlebar so the rear wheel lands first. *(Courtesy Kawasaki Motor Corp.)*

There's a good chance that the front wheel will be twisted to the side, wrenching the handlebar from your grasp. That's the time when you become a participant in an "endo," or flip, over the handlebar.

If you ever ride over a series of bumps ("whoop-de-doos" to motocrossers) and you can't bring the front end of the bike up, slam on the rear brake and feather the throttle slightly, taking care that you don't completely close it. With the rear wheel dragging from brake application, it tends to fall into line with the front wheel to keep the motorcycle from acting like a bucking bronc.

Although it's beyond the scope of this chapter to get into the advanced methods used in motocross and other forms of off-road competition, it does attempt to give you some fundamental techniques that can help you later. Once you learn to control a motorcycle in the dirt, applying specific techniques becomes a must if you wish to compete.

Because off-road terrain is so varied, the latter part of this chapter has been set up to show you how to handle the most common kinds of terrain you'll encounter. Each kind has unique characteristics to tax your skills. After all, that's what makes dirt riding so challenging.

Sand

If there's a secret to maintaining traction in sand, it's to keep moving as fast as you can. Pull as high a gear as possible, and keep body weight to the rear, to keep the front end light so that the front wheel doesn't plow into the sand. Also, keep your arms limber. Don't be afraid to let the bike wander a little. Remember: you can always relieve some of the pressure on the arms by gripping the gas tank between the knees.

When changing gears, throw fast shifts. Don't roll the throttle back any more than necessary, because weight transference to the front wheel when the bike slows will make it dig into the sand more.

What is difficult at first in sand riding is to attempt to corner. The last thing you want to do is to brake into a turn, because weight transference will make that front tire really dig in and slide. If you're in a higher gear as you set up for the turn, downshift as rapidly as possible, to keep the engine revs from dropping off too much. Keep your weight to the rear. Just shutting off the throttle for an instant will help to set the bike up for a turn.

One of the real challenges of sand riding is trying to get out of a sandwash. Use your feet to push the bike, as you rev up the engine and engage the clutch. As soon as you get moving, yank the feet up on the footrests and zip into second gear.

If you stay in low gear too long, all you'll get for your trouble is a deeper ditch for your rear tire. By getting into a higher gear as soon as possible, the rear tire can take more advantage of the less-frequent power pulses from the engine.

In fact, in any kind of cross-country running, the higher the gear you run in, the easier it is to handle the bike.

For optimum traction in the sand, you want the knobbiest tire possible, although trials-universals work well, if they're wide enough. Tire pressure should be about one half or less than that used for on the road.

Mud and Water

As in sand, negotiating mud successfully has a lot to do with momentum. If you can keep moving fast enough without inducing wheelspin and destroying that critical traction point at the rear tire, you'll get through mud all right.

Body English enters into mud riding, as sensitive balance becomes necessary to maintain traction at the rear tire's contact point. By standing on the footrests, you gain much better balance and traction.

If the mud is the shallow-clay, hard-base type, tenderly operate the throttle and leave the clutch alone to get better traction. When moving uphill in this type of mud, you might have to "crank open" the engine in second gear to let the rear tire break through.

The other kind of mud you can expect to encounter is gumbo. Its seemingly bottomless composition can bog you down quickly, if you don't maintain enough momentum. The only effective way to navigate it is to keep those feet on the footrests, weight to the rear, and power on. Once you lose forward speed, you sink. And then you have to pry your bike out.

Here's how to do it: you push your pride and joy over on its side, then you grab the lower part of it and push it over again until it's resting on the handlebar and gas tank. You keep pushing, and pushing, until you get it on firm ground. By that time, your machine is a blob of mud.

Gumbo tends to pack into the most undesirable places. For that reason, you need high fenders, so it can't pack up between the fenders and wheels and bring the machine to a halt. Where the front fender is mounted close to the wheel, a mud-catching device can be mounted on the lower part of the fender to scrape mud off the tire. Such a device fitted over the rear chain is also a good idea, or else the chain will act like a conveyer belt as it carries mud back to the gearbox sprocket to pack it in and jam the sprocket.

Sometime or another during your off-road jaunts, you'll find yourself wrestling with the idea of crossing water. Rule one is don't attempt to scoot across without conducting some kind of preride inspection of your intended path. If you can't see bottom where you intend to cross, park the bike and walk across first. Sure, you'll get your feet wet, but you're better off discovering a sudden drop-off by walking into it rather than falling into it with your bike.

Once you've decided the safest route, you then have to decide how to ride your bike. If it's a wide body of water with a fairly smooth bottom, you can sit and keep the feet poised just above the water, in case you need to catch your bike from falling over. A mud bottom will require more forward speed than a rock-bed bottom. Slimy stones will demand that you use Body English and stand on the footrests. You'll have to develop a sensitive touch on the controls, too.

Keep the engine revved up in case water finds its way into the electrical system and causes the engine to skip a beat or two. Should you be unlucky enough to drop Old Paint in the water, shut the engine off immediately. Water is incompressible. If enough of it gets sucked into the carburetor, it can blow off the cylinder head or cave in a piston.

How to Handle Hills

No other aspect of dirt riding can provide you with more thrills (or scares) than riding hills. It's important that you don't let a steep hill psyche you out. If you become fearful of it, you're going to have more difficulty in climbing it than if you just viewed it as another piece of terrain.

When it comes to climbing a hill successfully, momentum is where it's at. Before climbing a hill, first study it to see just what path you can take with the least fuss.

You might have to deviate from a straight line to avoid deep ruts or loose stones, but traction is what you want. A straight line might be the shortest distance between two points as the crow flies, but you're no crow.

Once you've assessed the route you're going to take, you're ready to point that front wheel toward the sky.

If the bike is geared low enough and you can build up some momentum before hitting the base of the hill, you might be able to go up in second gear. With your weight on the footrests, lean forward on the handlebar to keep the bike from flipping over on you. As the slope gets steeper, you might have to downshift into low gear to maintain traction.

If you start to bog down, you've gotten into one of those situations where it's excusable to use your feet to "paddle." Before going over the top, shut off the throttle. You don't want to continue once you reach the top unless you know what's on the other side.

However, if you should come to a halt before you reach the top, don't panic and scream for help. Instead, slap on the brakes and lay the bike on its side.

Now you have two alternatives: you can either try to go on, or you can work the bike around and go back down.

Let's consider alternative number one first. If you've stopped because the rear tire dug itself into a ditch, kick some dirt or stones into the rut to give the rear tire something to bite on. Then climb back on, take a deep breath, and perform the following actions simultaneously: push forward on the handlebar, paddle and push with your feet, gas it, and pop the clutch. If this pushing/paddling/gassing/popping doesn't help, you might try "walking" the bike up. As you lean against the side of the motorcycle, let the clutch out gingerly and push forward on the handlebar at the same time. In this situation, activate the throttle with the pocket between the thumb and forefinger, while you apply the front brake. Once the clutch engages, get off the brake.

If, despite all this effort, you still can't make it up, resort to alternative number two: going down. Dismount and lay the bike on its side. With the front brake dragging, let the machine drift backward a little, while you turn the handlebar to the side you're standing. The technique here is to get the bike sideways on the hill, with yourself positioned on the *topside* of the hill. This way, if the bike should roll over, you'll be above it. Once you have the bike sideways, you can work the handlebar back and forth, until the bike is pointing downward. You have a choice of ways that you can descend. If you have unlimited courage, jump on and race down kamikaze style. Here you stand a good chance of ending up in a crumpled pile at the bottom of the hill. But if you're like most "descenders," you'll use a little more discretion. Before starting down, you'll study the hill (again) to see if the path you took going up is as good for going down. During your climb, you may have changed the surface somewhat, so don't assume that it'll always be okay to follow the same track in both directions.

Downhill technique varies among dirt riders. Some daring souls will put the gearbox in neutral and lock the rear brake. But the danger here is that the rear tire will skid, with the result that the rear end of the bike will try to beat the front end down the hill.

The best way to descend a steep hill is to get into first gear (with clutch engaged), stand on the footrests with your weight to the rear, and shut off the engine. Some riders, however, prefer to keep the engine ticking over.

If the base of the hill doesn't have a smooth radius, brace your arms so the front wheel doesn't catch and twist the handlebar from your grasp when it rolls onto the radius. If you have to apply the brakes to slow your descent, use equal amounts of application, front and rear. It's best not to use any brake, though. But some riders drag the front brake, while they also drag their feet.

If you have a four-stroke single with a compression release, you have an advantage in that you can slow your descent considerably. By shutting off the engine, selecting low gear, and operating the compression release, the engine will function like an air pump to increase the engine's retarding effect on the rear wheel. Should you find yourself still descending too fast, apply the rear brake only and lay the bike over on the uphill side to bring it to a sliding halt. After you get it under control again, you can proceed to descend as originally intended.

Riding up and down hills strewn with rocks demands the ultimate in finesse. To maintain control, stand on the footrests and let the bike move around underneath you. Don't lean or pull on the handlebar. Balance yourself on the footrests so your arms are kept loose enough to flick the front wheel between rocks. It's imperative that you keep the rear tire from breaking loose. Depending how rocky the path is when going uphill, you'll probably have to slip the clutch often and rev the engine considerably.

Make sure the clutch is up to such rigors.

When descending a fairly steep rocky path, use only the rear brake. If you use the front brake, it'll tend to make the tire push the rocks away rather than ride over them. A rock doesn't have to move very far with the front tire resting on it to cause a spill. You can use the front brake, however, if a rock the front tire is on is a large one. Also, you can apply the front brake where there's solid ground between rocks.

You can drag the rear brake going down, but if it slides the rear tire, let off. Remember: when ascending or descending rocky hills, take time to thoroughly study your planned route.

We've looked at riding up and down hills. What about riding across them? How do you do that without sliding down? The recommended technique here is to stand on the footrests, with the body weight concentrated on the downhill footrest. This action forces the tires into the side of the hill more, to permit better traction. Go easy on the gas and brakes. Any sudden disturbance to those tires' contact points will make them break loose. Guess what happens then?

As tricky as it is to come down hills, it can be even trickier to descend mini-hills or ledges. The idea of going over a steep ledge can throw more fear into some dirt riders than that of coming down a long hill.

When learning ledge jumping, don't tackle any that are beyond your ability.

Before you "jump off" a ledge, pull your front wheel up to the edge and look it over. The drop-off height should be shorter than your bike's wheelbase, with a smooth gentle radius at the bottom. If everything looks all right, nudge the front wheel over the edge and get in low gear. Feather the front brake and apply some rear brake. Your gearshift foot should be on the ground for balance.

Let the machine roll forward until the skidplate brushes against the corner of the ledge. Then plant both feet against the ledge and thrust the bike over the rest of the way.

As the motorcycle starts down, let off the front brake and close the throttle. You might leave your feet off the footrests to act as stabilizers. And push against the handlebar to keep your weight rearward. Keep that two-wheeler moving in a straight line and brace your arms for the abrupt transition from vertical to horizontal at the bottom.

Log Jumping

You won't ride very far in the woods before you come across a fallen tree or a discarded log. If there's room enough, go around it. But when you're riding down a narrow path and there's no room, you have no choice but to go over it. Once you get the hang of it, log jumping is fun. But you have to know what you're doing. To learn log jumping, start out with those that have a diameter of no more than six or eight inches.

Approach a log at a right angle, as you would a railroad crossing. The difference with the log is that it's a lot higher than a rail. Your speed should be slow, with the bike in first gear. If the log has never been crossed before, its bark will provide good traction. But if the bark has been worn off, the undersurface will be slippery, particularly if it's wet. If the front tire hits that undersurface at an angle, it'll end up sliding along the log instead of going over it.

Just before the front tire makes contact with the log, force your weight down on the footrests to compress the suspension units. Then yank your body up away from the footrests and handlebar to lighten the load on the bike. Be sure you don't let go of the handlebar and come off the footrests.

When you jerk your weight upward, the suspension units extend and the bike acts as though it's lighter. Once the front tire hits the log, it "floats" over it.

For bigger logs, the best way to get over is to get the front end to come up in a "wheelie" position. When the front wheel is about a foot from the log, gas the engine and tug up on the handlebar. After the front wheel gets over the log, roll the throttle off and let the front end drop as the rear tire

Once the rear tire has started climbing over the log, body weight should be placed rearward to keep the rear end of the bike from springing up into the air. *(Courtesy Yamaha International Corp.)*

contacts the log. As the rear tire climbs the log, bend your knees (while still standing) and lean forward. By pushing the bike forward, it becomes easier for the rear wheel to climb the log. As the rear wheel comes over, turn on the throttle.

If the log is large, the bike might get hung up on its skidplate. And if you don't have enough momentum to get over, the bike will seesaw forward and backward. The rear tire must get traction against the log, or you're not going anywhere, unless you lunge forward hard enough to get the front end to drop so the rear tire can bite against the log.

When You Come to a Dead End

Sometimes you'll ride into narrow areas that come to dead ends. If the ground slants steeply to either side and in front of you, the only way out may be the way you came in. And if you can't turn around, what do you do? Push your bike out backward? Possibly.

Or you might elect to stay on it and try this. Turn the front wheel toward the least-steep or least-rough side. Then, keeping your feet down for balance, climb up the slope just far enough that your feet are still in contact with the level ground. Pull in the clutch and let the bike drift backward, as you turn the handlebar to the side. It may take only one try to get you pointing out the way you came in. Or it may take several attempts. But eventually you'll get out.

As you near the end of your journey through this book, you've formed some impressions about it, whether you're aware of them at this moment or not. And a peculiarity of the written word is that you might not think any more about what you've read until you're exposed to a situation that you've read about.

Maybe this book will help you in this manner. Whether it helps you develop into the kind of rider you want to be depends on what you can extract from it. If you can make use of just one bit of information from this publication, would you say it has been of value to you? Only you can answer this.

In any event, the author's best wishes go with you, wherever you ride. So, climb on that two-wheeler and head out. A new world awaits you.

Index